VENISON

VENISON

A Complete Guide to Hunting, Field Dressing and Butchering, and Cooking Deer

Words
JOSÉ L. SOUTO

Camera
STEVE LEE

Introduction
KATE FIDUCCIA

Skyhorse Publishing

First Skyhorse Edition © 2020
First published in the United Kingdom as *Venison—the Game Larder* by Merlin Unwin Books Limited.
Text © 2015 Jose Souto
Photographs © 2015 Steve Lee (unless otherwise noted)
Introduction © 2020 Kate Fiduccia

Skyhorse Publishing books may be purchased in bulk at special discounts for sales promotion, corporate gifts, fund-raising, or educational purposes. Special editions can also be created to specifications. For details, contact the Special Sales Department, Skyhorse Publishing, 307 West 36th Street, 11th Floor, New York, NY 10018 or info@skyhorsepublishing.com.

Skyhorse® and Skyhorse Publishing® are registered trademarks of Skyhorse Publishing, Inc.®, a Delaware corporation.

Visit our website at www.skyhorsepublishing.com.

10 9 8 7 6 5 4 3

Library of Congress Cataloging-in-Publication Data is available on file.

Cover design by Mona Lin
Cover photo credit: Steve Lee

Print ISBN: 978-1-5107-6261-9
Ebook ISBN: 978-1-5107-6346-3

Printed in China

CONTENTS

INTRODUCTION

My love for preparing Mother Nature's natural grass-fed meat—venison—has spanned nearly four decades. During this time, I have hunted several of the species of deer throughout North America and have appreciatively prepared the bounty for many savory meals. Fortunately for today's venison lover, there are more ways to obtain this delicate treasure of the woods and learn how to prepare delicious domestically traditional and internationally acclaimed venison recipes.

Whether preparing a smaller species of deer, such as sika deer, or larger species such as elk, the composition of venison is similar and field care should be the same. The venison will taste best if the animal is shot while it is relaxed, and the carcass is field-dressed immediately after the animal is down. Subsequently, the carcass should then be rinsed free of any blood and debris and cooled down to minimize any bacterial growth. Keeping these simple, yet vital, steps as a must-do part of your hunting rules will vastly improve the taste of the meat.

Venison is a lean, red meat that most often is cooked low and slow or, for whole cuts, only to medium-rare. The sections of the animal that do the most work and have the most connective tissue, such as the neck and forelegs, should be slow-cooked, braised, marinated, or pressure cooked. These methods will break down the sinew, connective tissue and other tough muscle proteins. Other cuts like the loins, saddle, and hind legs or haunch, when they are not roasted, can be cooked to a medium-rare state. Keep in mind, if the recipe does not include any marinade prior to cooking, and it involves a high-heat method (such as grilling, searing, or pan frying), the venison will need to reach only a medium-rare state to maintain its flavor and texture.

Venison is a showcase for Chef Jose L. Souto's passion for deer, butchering, preparing venison, and his love to share his sage knowledge through his very popular game seminars as Chef Lecturer in Culinary Arts at Westminster Kingsway College in England. With six species of deer in the UK (red deer, roe deer, fallow deer, sika deer, Chinese water deer, and Reeves' muntjac) and virtually no natural predators, venison is abundant throughout the countryside. Fittingly, venison is a popular item in butchers' shops and is a common menu item in restaurants. Many of the finer restaurants in the UK differentiate between the species of deer and their provenance. *Venison* shares excellent on-point butchering instructions with clear, identifiable signs noting the various cuts that are typical to British venison preparation. Chef Souto is a master of his craft and leaves no stone unturned when showing step-by-step images of proper butchering techniques. The venison recipe photography and food styling by world-renowned expert Steve Lee is inspirational.

For more than twenty years I have been giving wild game cooking demos. If there is one common thread among the people I have met, it is that each one is always looking for new ways to prepare this delicious meat. For those of you who share this interest, what you are about to read will surely pique your curiosity. In addition to his own mouthwatering recipes, Chef Souto includes recipes from professional chefs, many of whom are hunters, as well as recipes from former students who have gone on to share the passion of and their respect for the preparation of venison. From Chef Jose Souto's Herb-Rolled Venison Loin with Chanterelle Mushrooms to celebrity chef Jun Tanaka's Venison Haunch cooked in a Spiced Salt Crust to Executive Chef Tom Egerton's Venison Scotch Eggs with Pickled Cucumber and Port-Poached Redcurrants, it will be hard to select which recipe to start with. If you love venison or are just beginning to venture with this all-natural game meat, you will enjoy the simple and delicious recipes shared by chefs whose respect for deer, the mastery of butchery and venison's provenance are unmatched.

Kate Fiduccia, author of *The Wild Game Cookbook, The Jerky Bible, Cabin Cooking*, and *The Venison Cookbook.*

White-tailed deer buck. *Photo Credit: Getty Images*

THE DEER SPECIES OF NORTH AMERICA

White-tailed deer (*Odocoileus virginianus*)

White-tailed deer (aka whitetail, Virginia deer) is a medium-sized deer that is native to North America, Central America, and South America all the way to Peru and Bolivia. It is even found in New Zealand, Cuba, Jamaica, Hispaniola, the Bahamas, the Lesser Antilles, and several European countries including Germany, the Czech Republic, Finland, Romania, France, and Serbia. In the Americas, the whitetail is the most widely distributed deer. Worldwide there are thirty-eight recognized subspecies of white-tailed deer.

Rut

The whitetail's breeding season begins when female deer (does) become fertile and receptive to amorous bucks. Across North America the genesis of the rut occurs in relationship with dates within the nine latitude zones (aka parallels) of Canada, the United States, and Mexico. Within each latitude, the rut takes place, whether it is cold or hot, with surprising regularity. The internal trigger of the rut is through the preorbital gland, located in the corner of each eye. It senses cycles of waning light levels, or photoperiods, that begin in autumn. As light decreases, more testosterone and other secretions are released and trigger a buck's brain to recognize the start of the breeding season.

Size and Weight

On average, a white-tailed deer is about two and a half to three and a half feet at the shoulder. The size of whitetails, however, can vary widely depending on where they live in North America. Generally, an adult male whitetail deer weighs 150 to 300 pounds. Some bucks, though, have been documented at live weights more than 400 pounds. Does averagely weigh between 90 to 200 pounds. Larger deer tend to inhabit more northerly climates, while smaller deer tend to live in warmer, more southern climates.

Antlers

Adult whitetail bucks regrow a set of branching antlers with eight to ten points every year. Immature bucks grow a single antler on each side of the head, called spikes. The spikes can be long or very short.

Description and Foods

A whitetail's coat is reddish-brown in spring and summer. In fall and winter the coat is grey-brown. Whitetails are instantly recognized by the distinctive white color on the underside of the tail. An indication of the age of a whitetail is the length of the muzzle and the darkness of its coat. Mature deer generally have longer snouts and dark gray coats.

White-tailed deer forage on a wide variety of wild plants, grasses, shoots, leaves, legumes, acorns, fruit, mushrooms, and even poison ivy. Whitetails are opportunistic feeders eating whatever becomes ripe and available. They have even been known to occasionally feed on insects and mice. The white-tailed deer is a ruminant that has a four-chambered stomach with each chamber performing a specific and different function. It allows the deer to eat fast and digest what it eats later, in a safe area of cover.

Flavor of Meat

White-tailed deer meat has a slight gamey flavor. Like any wild game animal, its flavor and tenderness are totally dependent on the animal's diet. Whitetails taken from agricultural lands often lack any detectable gamey taste.

Mule Deer (*Odocoileus hemionus*)

Mule deer (aka mulie), like wapiti, are considered icons of the American West. They are found throughout western North America, from the coastal islands of Alaska, to the West coast, in the Great Plains, the southern Yukon Territory, and the western Canadian provinces of British Columbia, Alberta, and Saskatchewan.

Rut

Mule deer subspecies are found in central Mexico to almost the Arctic Circle. In the United States, they range from the West Coast to the midwestern prairies. Mule deer breeding periods vary significantly. In the far northern reaches of the mule deer's range, the rut can start as early as mid-October and run into December. In the mid to lower Rocky Mountains, where mule deer are most plentiful, the breeding season generally starts at the beginning of November. In the Southwestern deserts, the rut generally starts in mid-December and can last to the beginning of January.

Size and Weight

Mule deer are generally larger than whitetails. They are about three to three and a half feet at the shoulder and five to seven feet long. Bucks weigh on average between 130 to 280 pounds, but some can be much heavier. Does weigh considerably less, averaging about 120 to 190 pounds.

Antlers

An adult mule deer buck has antlers with main beams that sweep outward and upward, forking once and then forking a second time. Brow tines are usually small and sometimes absent altogether. Male bucks usually have 10 points that include small brow tines of an inch or more. In the West, a buck's antlers are counted on one side excluding the brow tines; therefore a buck with 10 points is referred to as a 4-point buck.

Description and Foods

Mule deer are easily identified by their large mule-like ears. Mule deer generally have a distinctive black forehead that contrasts sharply with a light grey face. The lighter facial coloration helps to make the eye rings and muzzle markings less obvious. The mule deer coat color is brownish-grey. Its rump has a white patch with a small white tail that is black at the tip. Mule deer are primarily browsers, with most of their diet comprised of forbs, leaves, twigs, and woody shrubs. In agricultural areas they eat corn, alfalfa, soybeans, and other agricultural plants. They also consume some nuts and fruits where and when they are ripe and available.

Flavor of Meat

Mule deer meat generally doesn't have a "gamey" flavor. If the deer has a diet high in sage brush, however, the meat will not be very tasty. It's all about an animal's diet. Good food, good eating. Sage brush--not so good eating!

Photo Credit: Getty Images

Coues Deer (*O. v. couesi*)

The Coues deer, native to Arizona, is a subspecies of the white-tailed deer. Coues deer (aka fantail deer) are small, desert-dwelling deer. Their habits, food items and the landscape which they inhabit set them apart from the white-tailed deer. They are also found in parts of New Mexico. The best populations and hunting are in Mexico. Coues deer are hunted in much the same manner as whitetails.

Rut

The Coues' rut activity really kicks into gear in December, making bucks more visible to hunters as the males seek and chase does. Coues bucks tend to gather harems and stick with them, much like bull elk do. Coues bucks will gather a group of does and work to keep other competitive bucks from stealing any females from the harem. A Coues buck spends a lot of time and energy chasing and fighting off satellite bucks.

Size and Weight

The Coues whitetail is sometimes called an elf or tiny deer. They stand about thirty-two to thirty-four inches at the shoulder. A mature buck seldom exceeds one hundred pounds live weight, although some may weigh slightly more than that.

Antlers

Coues deer have branching antlers that compare identically to those of whitetail bucks. Adult Coues bucks have antlers of 8 points or more, although the antlers are much smaller than typical white-tailed buck antlers. A buck grossing 100 Boone & Crockett points is considered to have a good set of antlers by most experienced Coues deer enthusiasts. Antlers that score more than 100 B&C points are trophy-class. Comparatively, most adult whitetail bucks will score 130 B&C inches, with trophy buck antlers scoring 160 B&C inches.

Description and Foods

Coues have ears and tails that appear to be out of proportion to their small body sizes. Their hides are generally lighter in hue than those of white-tailed deer and other deer species. Coues eat mostly browse, acorns from desert oaks and fruit from atop barrel cacti.

Flavor of Meat

The texture and tenderness of Coues' deer meat is said to be comparable to veal. It's tender, lean, and pleasantly flavorful. It lacks any distinct unpleasant gamey taste. However, it shouldn't be compared to any domestic meats—particularly veal.

Photo Credit: Getty Images

3

Sitka Black-tailed Deer (*Odocoileus hemionus sitkensis*)

The Sitka black-tailed deer (*Odocoileus hemionus sitkensis*) are smaller, stockier, and have shorter faces than other members of the black-tailed group. Sitka black-tailed deer are closely related to the larger Columbia black-tailed deer of the Pacific Northwest, and both are believed to be subspecies of the larger mule deer of the American West. Found mostly in coastal rainforests of Southeast Alaska and north-coastal British Columbia, their range has been expanded to include populations near Yakutat, Prince William Sound, and on Kodiak and Afognak islands.

Rut

November is generally an excellent time to hunt Sitka black-tailed deer. They usually begin rutting by the first of November, with the rut usually peaking by mid-month.

Size and Weight

The average live weight of an adult Sitka black-tailed buck is about 120 pounds, but some bucks have been reported to weigh more than two hundred pounds. Female Sitka deer generally weigh about eighty pounds.

Antlers

Sitka black-tail buck antlers are generally dark brown with typical whitetail and black-tailed branching. An adult buck's antler development is usually three points on each side. The antlers are relatively small, with very few scoring more than 110 points by the Boone & Crockett system.

Description and Foods

The color of a summer coat of Sitka black-tailed deer is reddish-brown and turns dark brownish-gray in fall and winter. Sitka deer are herbivorous and, as such, feed

Photo Credit: Getty Images

on vegetation and green leaves of shrubs, along with evergreen forbs and woody browse.

Flavor of Meat

Sitka venison is a strong-flavored dark meat, but it's not a disagreeable taste. In fact, it is often described as tasting like elk meat.

Elk (*Cervus canadensis*)

Elk (aka Wapiti) is the second largest species within the deer family, Cervidae. There are four subspecies of elk in North America: the Roosevelt, Tule, Manitoban, and Rocky Mountain. Each subspecies inhabits different areas within North America. Rocky Mountain elk have the largest antlers of all four elk subspecies and are the most heavily hunted of elk. They inhabit sections of Alaska, Washington, Oregon, California, Arizona, Utah, Colorado, Wyoming, Idaho, Montana, Nevada, New Mexico, North Dakota, South Dakota, Michigan, Minnesota, Oklahoma, Kentucky, Pennsylvania, Arkansas, and Texas.

Rut

The peak of the Rocky Mountain elk breeding period is generally mid-September to mid-October. During the rut, a herd of a dozen or more cow elk are closely guarded by one dominant bull elk. Herd bulls are frequently challenged by other adult bulls and lesser dominant satellite bulls that are looking to steal cows. The goal of a herd bull is to prove his prowess and earn the loyalty of his harem of cows by fighting off any challengers. Most herd bulls are about eight to nine years old and stand the best chance of mating.

Size and Weight

A mature Rocky Mountain bull elk weighs about seven hundred pounds and stands five feet tall at the shoulder. A cow elk weighs about five hundred pounds and stands four and a half feet at the shoulder.

Antlers

A mature bull generally has 6 points on each antler and is known as a 6-by-6. A 12-point bull (6x6) with antlers measuring 260 to 290 Boone & Crockett inches is considered a trophy. Bulls with 6x6 antlers measuring 325 to 340 B&C inches are regarded as prized trophy bull elk. An 6x6 is called a "royal"; a 7x7 bull is referred to as an "imperial," and a bull sporting a rare set of 16 points (8x8) is titled a "monarch."

Description and Foods

Since elk are primarily grazing animals, they prefer to eat grasses in large open meadows. They also browse on aspen and oak leaves and a variety of other plants found in their environment. Elk are twice as large as mule deer. They have a reddish hue to their hide and distinctive large, buff-colored rump patches and smaller tails. Bulls have distinctively shaped antlers that sweep over the back of the bull's body almost to its rump.

Flavor of Meat

Elk flesh is very tender and flavorful, and does not need marinating. Its taste is often said to be a little more flavorful than other deer, just enough to know you're eating something special. With wild elk, and especially farm-raised elk, you never have to worry that the meat will taste gamey.

Photo Credit: Getty Images

Photo Credit: Getty Images

Moose (*Alces alces*)

Moose of North America are members of the New World subfamily of deer. There are three subspecies of moose, including the Alaska-Yukon moose, the Canadian moose (Western and Eastern), and the Shiras Moose. Moose are the largest and heaviest species within the family of Cervidae. They generally inhabit boreal and coniferous forests that include lakes, ponds, rivers, and other waterways. Most large populations of moose are found in Canada, Alaska, Yukon, and New England. The Shiras moose is found in a few western states including Colorado, Utah, Montana, and Wyoming. Maine has the highest population of Eastern moose within the lower forty-eight states. The province of Newfoundland and Labrador has the densest population of Eastern moose in North America. The Eastern moose is the most hunted of the three subspecies of moose; they are mostly hunted in Newfoundland.

Rut

Generally, the peak of the rutting season for moose takes place from the last week of September through the first two weeks of October. In Alaska and the Yukon Territory, the rut happens mostly in September. In Maine and the states in the West, the rut typically takes place in October. For the most part, early October will be the peak.

Size and Weight

Moose are the largest and heaviest of all deer in North America. An Alaska-Yukon bull moose stands more than seven feet at the shoulder and weighs more than 1,400 pounds. The Eastern bull moose stands about six feet at the shoulder and weighes about 1,400 pounds. A Shiras bull moose can reach an amazing seven feet tall at the shoulder and can be ten feet long. A mature Shiras bull moose weighs about 600 to 1300 pounds.

Antlers

The antlers of an Alaskan-Yukon bull moose span about six feet, while the antlers of the Eastern bull span of about five feet across. The antlers of a Shiras bull moose can also span five feet wide. The paddles (antlers) of a full-grown bull moose can weigh between forty and fifty pounds.

Description and Foods

During the late fall and winter, moose eat a variety of twigs. Other times of the year they graze on leaves, bark, pine cones, buds, and shrubs. They also eat aquatic plants such as water lilies. Moose are easily identifiable by their sheer size, antlers, and the black coloring of their hide.

Flavor of Meat

Moose meat is rated as the very best wild game deer meat. Properly prepared, it is said to be compared to beef. It is tender and flavorful. Only the bison is said to be a better tasting wild game meat. If a bull is killed during the peak of the rut, however, the meat can be slightly chewy.

Caribou reindeer (*Rangifer tarandus*)

The reindeer in North America is called a caribou. It is a species of deer with circumpolar distribution, native to Arctic, sub-Arctic, tundra, boreal, and mountainous regions of North America. There are three subspecies of North American caribou: (*Rangifer t. caribou*); the Barren Ground (*Rangifer t. granti*) caribou; and the Woodland (*Rangifer tarandus caribou*).

Rut

The rut for Alaska caribou generally takes place the last two weeks of September to the first two weeks of October. Bull caribou sometimes ingest urine from cow caribou during the rut, oftentimes tainting the meat so badly it can't be eaten. Not all bulls come into rut at the same time, however, and killing a non-rutting bull will provide untainted meat.

Size and Weight

Adult bulls can weigh about 350-400 pounds, sometimes more. Caribou in northern and southwestern Alaska are generally smaller than caribou in the interior and southern parts of the state.

Antlers

The antlers of adult bull caribou are large and massive. Female caribou also grow antlers, but they are spindly and much smaller than the antlers of the males.

Description and Foods

In late fall, caribou hides are clove-brown with a white neck, rump, and feet, and often have a white flank stripe. Caribou eat the leaves of willows, sedges, flowering tundra plants, and mushrooms. In September they switch to lichens, dried sedges, and small shrubs (like blueberry).

Flavor of Meat

Caribou meat is a tasty alternative when the caribou is killed before or after the rut. The meat is lean, but like all deer it doesn't have the marbling found in beef. Caribou meat can be as tender as moose or elk meat.

Photo Credit: Getty Images

BUTCHERING THE CARCASS

SKINNING

Once the carcass has cooled down and been hung, we need to skin it. So first ensure you have a secure hanging point where you can put weight on the carcass as you remove the skin.

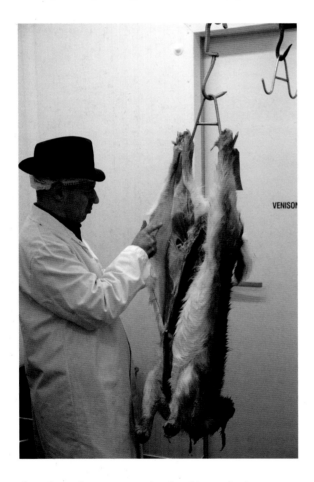

Start by making a cut under the skin on the inner thigh up towards the haunch then with the tip of the knife, work the skin off the flesh.

Work down the belly and breast holding the knife flat and cutting between the skin and the flesh. Be careful not to cut into the flesh or, later, when you come to pull on the skin it will tear the flesh. Take this cut down to the shoulder, then repeat on the other side. Be careful to turn the skin over onto itself so that the fur does not come into contact with the clean carcass.

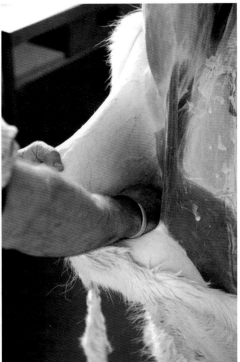

Left: Once you have done both sides, take hold of the skin in one hand and form a fist with the other then roll your fist between skin and flesh: this is called 'punching out'. Punch the skin out until you come to the shoulder.

Below left: Once you have all the skin punched out down to the shoulder, make a cut along the inside of the shoulder then pull the skin down on both sides and around the end of the shoulder.

Below: Once the skin is removed, wipe the carcass down with a dry cloth to remove any unwanted fur.

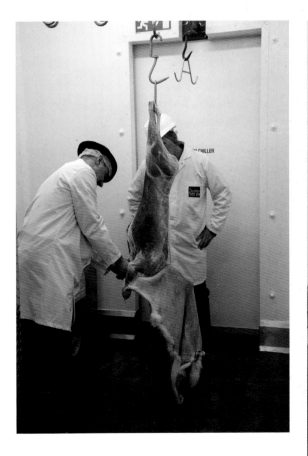

Once the carcass has been skinned and wiped down to rid it of any unwanted hair we can begin to break it down into primal joints. Here we have a fallow deer showing the main joints into which we can divide the carcass: the shoulder, the breast, the scrag (or neck), the fillets, the long saddle and, finally, the haunch.

SHOULDER

Let's start with the shoulder.

Take hold of the shoulder and pull it out, away from the main carcass. As you pull the shoulder away you will see that a piece of meat attaches the shoulder to the carcass on its underside: in the armpit, if you like. Make an incision here and as you cut, carry on pulling the shoulder away from the carcass. There is no bone here so you will find no resistance. Follow the cut around the top of the shoulder and around the shoulder blade until the whole shoulder comes off. Repeat the same process on the other side.

BREAST

Now to remove the breasts. Follow the inside line of the haunch to where the leg meets the breast. Make a cut around the leg until you are 3 inches from the inner fillet. Mark a line along the side of the carcass then saw through the bones with a saw.

SCRAG OR NECK *(top)*

To remove the scrag or neck, cut around the base of the neck with a knife and then saw through the bone.

FILLETS *(center)*

The fillets are the only cut of meat on the inside of the carcass. They are situated on the inside of the backbone. Run your knife along the inside of the backbone along the fillet, starting at the top of the filet between the inside of the legs. Keeping the knife close to the bone, cut and peel the filet away from the bone.

LONG SADDLE *(below)*

To remove the long saddle, feel for the hip or pelvic bone between the haunch and the saddle, then run your knife across the back of the carcass just below the pelvic bone. Using a saw, cut through the bone carefully.

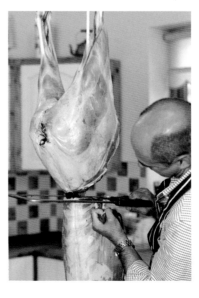

HAUNCH

Remove the two haunches from the gambrel and lay it on a board and place the tip of your boning knife into the hole between the haunches so that it is embedded in the backbone. Pull the knife toward you and you will reach a joint of cartilage between the haunches. Once you hit this, the knife will cut through the cartilage easily. If at first you do not hit the cartilage replace the knife and try again. Once you are through the cartilage, take a saw and cut along the backbone to divide the haunches.

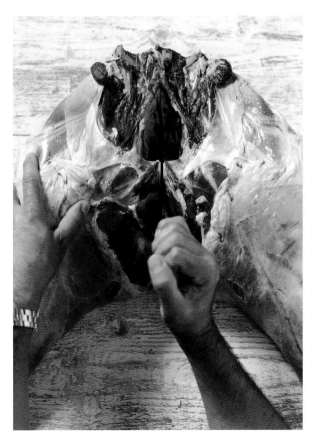

13

THE SHOULDER

The shoulder has many uses: as a whole braising joint, diced in stews and for mince. It is a tough joint that works hard and has plenty of flavor. The shoulder can be larded with fat to help it stay moist during cooking.

DE-BONING THE SHOULDER

1 Lay the shoulder on the table with the inside facing you.

2 With your fingers, starting at the foot end, feel up the shoulder and along the bone, to the first joint at the elbow, flexing the joint once you've found it.

3 Next move further up the shoulder and feel for the second joint.

4 Then feel along down from the second joint. At this point you will feel a large flat-shaped bone - this is the shoulder blade.

5 Place your knife at the top of the shoulder blade where you found the second joint and cut a line straight down the center of the blade bone. Work under the meat either side of the blade bone and around the edge.

6 As you work your way around the bone, you will see that the blade bone juts out toward the skin on the underside. Carefully work around the tip of the bone, working from both ends.

7 Once you have loosened the blade bone, place your knife on the second joint and this time make a cut from the second joint to the first joint at the elbow and then cut around and along the bone.

8 Once you have exposed the bone, cut through the second joint and remove the blade bone, then cut through the first joint to remove the second bone.

9 To keep it as a whole joint, I like to leave the end bone intact, just trimming the meat around it and sawing it straight, so this will give a handle to hold when cutting the joint.

10 The shoulder can then be stuffed and tied.

CUTS & JOINTS FROM THE SHOULDER

The whole shoulder on the bone:

This joint contains a lot of sinew and collagen and is a part of the animal that works hard, so it needs slow long cooking to break it down. In many rustic recipes it is cooked whole so that the meat is just falling off the bone.

The whole boned-out shoulder:

Boned and tied or stuffed and tied, this is a slow-cooking joint that will eventually become beautifully tender and full of flavor.

Mince & dice:

All the shoulder meat makes good mince and dice. The mince can be used for sausages, burgers and meat sauces such as Bolognese, and the dice can be used for stews, pies and puddings. Remember that shoulder is a tough part of the carcass so cook dice slow and long.

THE BREAST

The breast is a much-overlooked cut of venison. It might lack form, being a little flat, but it has great flavor and many uses.

BONING OUT THE BREAST

1 Running a boning knife along the middle of the rib bones, score along each one from top to bottom then, using your finger nails, pull the membrane from the middle of the bone where you have scored it, outwards, exposing the bone.

2 Once the tip of the bone is exposed, curl your finger around it and pull the bone out. It will pop out at a small joint at the base of each bone. Repeat this with all the bones on the breast.

3 At the point where the rib bone popped out, take a boning knife and cut along the length of the breast, getting under the joint, to remove the bone that runs along the bottom of the breast and the cartilage that connects it all.

RIBS FOR BBQ

1   To prepare the breast for BBQ ribs, cut a straight line along the bottom of the ribs with a sharp knife.

2   Taking a bone, saw cut along the line through the ribs and remove the bottom of the ribs. This bone can be used for stocks and sauces.

CUTS & JOINTS FROM THE BREAST

Whole trimmed breast on the bone:

This joint is flavorsome but can be tough and needs long, slow cooking. By removing the long bone and cartilage on the bottom of the breast, we can use it for braising and barbecues.

CUTS & JOINTS FROM THE BONED-OUT BREAST

Boned-out breast:

This can be cooked flat and cut, or stuffed, rolled and tied. Again, slow cooking is needed and do not over-stuff as this meat will shrink quite a lot.

Mince:

The breast is usually used for mince in burgers. It also makes good filling for sausages.

THE SCRAG

The scrag is a very under-utilised piece of meat. It is tough as it is one of the most worked muscles on the deer, therefore it has lots of flavor, sinew and collagen that will cook down to give a really delicious cut.

DE-BONING THE SCRAG

1   Run the boning knife from the top of the scrag on the back, to the bottom, just like you would follow the backbone on a long saddle.

2   Work your way around the neck to remove the meat on each side.

CUTS & JOINTS FROM THE SCRAG

De-boned scrag

The meat taken from either side of the scrag is full of flavor but it is also tough so needs long, slow cooking until it tenderises. Best cooked braised or sous vide (boil in a bag) for a long period of time. It can then be used as a piece or torn up, like pulled pork.

Scrag dice

Dice the scrag and use for stews. The collagen and sinew within the meat will keep it moist and enrich the sauce it is being cooked in.

LONG SADDLE

The long saddle is a tender, succulent joint which can be cut many different ways. But it is one of those cuts that chefs cannot seem to get away from. If you ask chefs for a venison recipe, most will go for the long saddle. This is a pity, as there are other cuts that are more flavorsome and equally tender. The long saddle can be boned into a cannon or split into best end and short saddle and cooked on the bone.

REMOVING THE LOIN

1   Starting at the top of the saddle and following the backbone, cut along it all the way down.

2   As you get down to the bottom of the saddle, work along the flat bones of the short saddle then along the curved bones of the best end, and finally along the middle neck.

3   Once you have removed the loin from the bone, lay it on the board upside-down then, using your fingers, feel along the eye of the meat and prise it from the skin.

4   Once the eye has come off, trim away all the sinew from the underside.

5   Using a filleting knife, remove the silver skin from the loin, as if you were skinning a fish.

6   Trim away all the sinew so that you have a solid eye of meat.

THE FILLET

The filet is one of the smallest joints on the carcass. On some deer such a muntjac, CWD and roe, they are tiny but in others such as red, sika and fallow they are more sizeable and, in culinary terms, of more use. I like to use the fillets of the larger deer for carpaccio and tartare because it is the most tender cut and is easy to digest. Chefs sometimes refer to the loin as the filet but this is strictly speaking not right as they are two different muscles in two very different places. Many chefs will also use the loin for carpaccio and tartare dishes but with the exception of roe loin, which is very tender, this is a mistake as the loin is a tougher muscle in large deer and is harder to digest. Our bodies have lost a lot of their ability to digest raw meat so, if we choose to eat it, we should always go with the most tender joint.

PREPARING THE FILLET

1   Remove the chain which is the piece of sinewy meat either side of the fillet.

2   Taking care not to remove too much meat, skim away the silver skin sinew around the fillet. This all needs to be removed as it will not cook out quickly and, with the fast cooking appropriate to fillet, if left it will be tough and cause the filet to curl up when cooked.

3   The filet can be kept whole, cut into medallions or into strips for a stir fry. If the deer is one of the larger species, the filet can be made into carpaccio.

THE BEST END

The Best End is where you'll find the cutlets and racks. Venison has varying layers of fat on it, depending on the time of year and the individual animal. Best Ends which have a little fat on them will cook well - keep the meat well basted. If there is no fat then you may want to remove the sinew on the outside of the cutlets or rack.

THE BEST END FOR CUTLETS AND RACK

1. Take the long saddle and place your knife by the last rib bone. Make a cut across the long saddle on both sides then saw through the backbone.

2. Count eight rib bones up on both sides of what you have left and again make a cut across the long saddle and saw through the backbone, creating three separate joints: the middle neck, the Best End, and saddle.

3. Cut along one side of the backbone down to where the ribs meet the backbone, pulling the meat back so that you cause a 2cm gap and you can see where the bones meet.

4. Turn the Best End over and, using a saw, make a cut where the bones meet to release the ribs away from the backbone.

5. Look at the eye of meat and measure it by placing your knife against it. Use this measurement to measure from the top of the eye toward the end of the rib-bone. Make a mark here and do the same at the other end along the back of the rack.

6. Join the two marks by cutting across the back ribs then cut the top end away by skimming the knife over the bones.

7. Cut away the meat between the ribs and then scrape each bone clean, and trim the bones so they are all square and the right length if you need to.

8. For a Rack: remove one bone at the neck end and then cut a cutlet from the neck end so that you get a nice clean cut. This will give you a 6-bone rack. On large deer, two bones per portion are enough; on smaller deer, three bones each. The rack is cooked whole then cut.

9. For Cutlets: remove one bone at the neck end and then cut a cutlet from the neck end, so that you get a nice clean cut. You now have six cutlets. Cut each one, making the cuts evenly between each bone.

THE SADDLE

The saddle is where all the flat bones are attached to the backbone. This is a joint that can be cut into chops which cook fantastically and quickly. I like to remove the outside skin on the saddle as it can be tough.

SADDLE FOR CHOPS

1   Place the saddle on the table with the inside of the backbone facing you. Saw down the middle of the backbone from top to bottom.

2   Remove the skin from the side you have taken off.

3   Wrap the whole joint in cling film and with a knife and saw, cut into 4cm-thick chops.

4   The filet could be left in the saddle and this will give you mini T-bone steaks.

CUTS & JOINTS FROM THE LONG SADDLE

From the Long Saddle:

The Loin: A joint loved by chefs as it produces full flavored, tender, perfectly round portions of meat which can be pan fried then roasted whole then sliced.

Cannons: Wrap the whole loin tightly in cling film so that you can cut 150-180g portions. Remove cling film then it can be pan fried then roasted whole, then cut in half or sliced.

Medallions: Wrap the whole loin tightly in cling film so that you can cut 25g slices. Remove cling film then it can be pan fried or flame grilled.

From the Fillet:

Whole Fillet: The whole filet can be used for carpaccio as it is the most tender cut of the whole carcass.

Tartare: The filet can be very finely diced NOT MINCED for tartare as it is a very tender, easily-digestible cut.

Stir fry: The filet can be cut into strips for stir fry.

From the Best End:

Racks: The best end can be divided into 2 x 8-bone racks that can be trimmed into 2 x 6-bone racks. These can be roasted whole then cut.

Cutlets: The racks can be divided into cutlets and pan fried or flame grilled.

From The Saddle:

Chops: The saddle can be cut into chops and flame grilled or pan fried.

THE HAUNCH

The haunch is venison's best known and most popular joint. A roast haunch is a fantastic joint but it can be difficult to cook. Here we have the preparation of the whole haunch for roasting and also the haunch broken down into individual muscle groups via seam boning. The main haunch joints are topside, silverside, shank, thick flank and the D-shaped rump.

PREPARING A WHOLE HAUNCH FOR ROASTING

1. Take the whole haunch and place onto your board with the inside of the leg face up. At the rump end of the haunch you will find the aitch-bone: this is one half of the pelvic bone which was cut in half when we split the two haunches in the carcass preparation.

2. With your finger, feel along the edge of the aitch-bone, then taking a boning knife, cut along the bone. Keep close to the bone which will guide you. When you reach the ball and socket joint, cut through it and open it out.

3. Cut behind and under the bone, removing it completely.

4. Go to the shank end now. Make a cut 10cm below the joint, cutting through the tendon, scrape the meat away to clean the bone and then saw through the shank bone. With the boning knife, scrape out the marrow bone from within the shank bone. This will help keep the end of the bone white during cooking.

5. Using butchers' twine, tie the joint up to keep it in one tight shape so that it will cook evenly. As venison contains very little fat, larger haunches could do with larding. This is where you place fat into the meat so that, as it cooks, the fat melts and bastes the meat. This can be done with a barding needle or with a boning knife. Make an incision by pushing the point of the knife into the muscle then pushing a piece of pork fat into the incision.

Small joints that make up the haunch

REMOVING THE SHANK AND RUMP FROM THE HAUNCH

The haunch can be cut into several joints to give individual portions or sharing portions. For professionals, it can also be a way of increasing profit and portions for your menu. Here are a few ways of doing this.

REMOVING THE SHANK

1   Take the haunch and remove the aitch-bone and trim the end of the shank bone (see point 4, roasting the whole haunch).

2   Feel along the bone, working from the end of the shank on the outside edge. Once you find the joint where the two bones meet, cut into it and make a straight cut across the meat. This will take you through cartilage joint.

REMOVING THE D-SHAPED RUMP

1   Take a large knife and make a cut 2cm below the ball joint, straight across.

OPEN-BONING THE HAUNCH FOR BARBECUE

A boned-out haunch is a great cut for a barbecue. With the bone removed, even the largest red deer haunch will cook in a very short time. The secret is to cut the meat so that it is all the same thickness, thereby minimising the cooking time.

1   Remove the shank and the aitch-bone from the haunch and then make a cut from the shank joint along the meat and bone to the ball joint at the other end.

2   Working around the bone with the knife, remove the bone completely.

3   Make a cut into the meat each side of where the bone was, so that the whole thing is the same thickness and has opened up like a book. This is sometimes known as a butterfly haunch.

REMOVING AND CLEANING THE SILVERSIDE & SALMON CUTS

1   Remove the shank and D-shaped rump then turn the haunch so that the outer part of the leg is facing you. Here you will see a white line that runs across the meat—this is a natural join in the muscle, make a cut along this and you will see that you are separating the muscles.

2   With your left hand pull the meat open only assisting it by cutting around the muscle not into it.

3   As you get to the other side of the muscle, cut it away: here you have the silverside, the larger joint and the salmon cut, the smaller joint.

4   Using your fingers, prise the two joints apart and then cut through the outer skin to separate them.

5   Remove all the sinew from around the silverside, the salmon cut has no sinew and can be left as it is.

REMOVING AND CLEANING THE TOPSIDE, BULLET & THICK FLANK

1   Carefully follow the bone from the top to the bottom of the joint and remove it by working your way around it then divide the joint into two where the bone was.

2   You will notice that the largest joint has a thin piece of meat that runs around the outside of it, this is the thin flank. Remove this by cutting along the seam and not into the muscle. Below this you will find two joints, the topside and the bullet.

3   You can separate these two joints with your fingers.

4   The joint on the other side also has an outer piece of meat that once removed will give you a round-shaped joint, this is the thick flank.

5   Remove any sinew from the outer parts of the joints carefully, as you will be pan frying, roasting or stir frying these joints. Any sinew on the outside of these joints will make them tough and curl up, as they do not have time to break down when cooking this way.

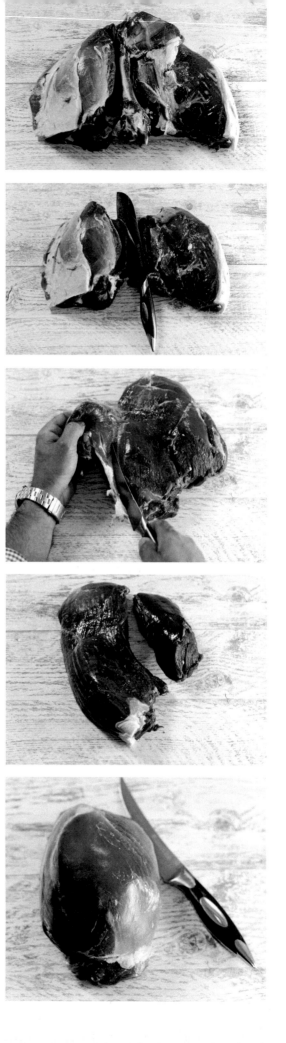

CUTS & JOINTS FROM THE HAUNCH

The Whole Haunch:

Whole Haunch: A classic roasting joint which is slow roasted and cooked no more than medium. It can be larded to give a little extra fat.

Open-Boned Haunch: A great joint to cook on a BBQ. It will not take long to cook and will be a fantastic centerpiece on the table.

From the Shank:

The Shank: a slow-cooking joint with lots of flavor, but one that will take time to cook. Do not rush it or it will go dry.

Osso Bucco: the shank cut through the bone into 4cm thick pieces: a slow-cooking cut with lots of flavor which takes a long time to cook. Do not rush it or it will go dry.

The Topside and Silverside:

Both these joints produce fantastic steaks. Cut them as small or large as you like, pan fry or flame grill them, but never cook to well done. The most you will want these is medium otherwise, because of the lack of fat, they will be dry and tough.

The Bullet and Salmon Cuts:

Both these joints are small and best used for a stir-fry or kebabs. They are tender as long as not over-cooked. The bullet has an artery halfway along that runs through the middle of the joint. Remove this before using.

The Thick Flank:

The thick flank can be used for steaks and also for paves. It's a cut used extensively and, dare I say, invented by my good friend Mike Robinson. These can be flame grilled or pan fried.

The D-Shaped Rump:

The rump can be left as a single sharing joint. The portions you will get depend on the size and species of deer. The rump can also be cut into portions but this can be wasteful, I think. It can be cooked as a slow-roast joint or as a pot roast.

The Off-Cuts:

The off-cuts and trimmings left from preparing the haunch will give you both dice or mince to use in a wide range of recipes.

MY RECIPES

As a chef I have over the years cooked venison in many different ways and here I am sharing a selection of some of those recipes.

The recipes I have included are a cross-section of easy as well as more challenging recipes. They combine many different ways of cooking as well as new ways of serving venison.

I hope you enjoy these recipes using a truly natural, healthy and sustainable product that is as versatile as it is flavorsome.

Happy cooking.

José L Souto

SMOKING & CURING

Smoking and curing are the old ways of preserving meat. Nowadays, these skills are no longer a necessity, due to refrigeration and freezing, but we have come to enjoy the flavor of smoked and cured products and we still choose to enjoy them today.

Smoking and curing also adds a new dimension to food and creates some ingenious products. Personally, I have produced venison bacon at Westminster Kingsway College for many years and have seen all manner of other products such as salamis, pastramis and chorizos taking venison to a whole new level. But these products are not cheap because they take time and effort to get right.

A chef can cook a dish and will have the fruits of his labour to taste and use within a short time but the production of charcuterie products needs time, patience and know-how.

For smoking I like to use a Bradley Smoker because they are efficient and they give a controllability to smoking that is second-to-none. They can be used for both hot and cold smoking.

These two methods of smoking are easily confused but are quite different:

- Cold smoking gives a smoky flavor and aroma to your product without cooking it, because there is no heat.

- Hot smoking cooks your product, adding a smoky flavor and aroma to your food but once the process is finished, the product can be eaten hot or chilled and eaten cold.

There are many woods available for smoking food, some stronger that others so choose wisely so as not to overpower your food. Bradley Smokers have a wide range of different choices.

There are a few rules to follow when smoking foods.

1   The surface of the food must be dry. This will allow the smoke to adhere to the food. If the surface is moist, the smoke will cause unsightly streaks on the food and will not smoke properly. I achieve thorough drying by allowing the product to sit in the fridge uncovered overnight. The air flow within the fridge helps to dry the surface of the meat.

2   Cleanliness is essential as these are ready-to-eat products.

3   When curing prior to smoking, the product needs to be given adequate time to cure and also to equalize which is when the product 'rests' as the salt is absorbed evenly throughout the meat. If this time is not adequate, when the cured meat is later cooked, the center will have a different color where the cure has not reached.

Throughout the recipe section there are some simple basic recipes for curing and smoking venison. Give them a try and you should get some great results.

Whole spit roast fallow with thyme and garlic

(WHOLE CARCASS)

Serves 25

WHOLE CARCASS

INGREDIENTS

MARINADE

2 bunches of thyme

2 heads of garlic, peeled

7 oz. Maldon salt

about 2 cups olive oil

It has long been an ambition of mine to cook a whole carcass of venison on a spit roast so when Steve came across the Winkleton Shoot shed, it was the perfect place to do it.

Whole deer cook well on a spit roast but be careful that the carcass is not too old or large. In this recipe I used a 33 lb. carcass (cleaned, skinned weight). You can go bigger by about 12 lb. but the larger the carcass, the longer it will take to cook and the longer it spends on the spit, the drier it will become.

As we know venison contains very little fat so it is good to marinate or oil the carcass to prevent over-drying. If you have an automatic gas spit, a 33 lb. carcass will take around 3 hours. A manual, log-fired spit will take slightly longer, about 4 hours. In either case the carcass should not be too close to the flames or the flames too high, as this will dry the meat out quickly and burn it before it is cooked. A 33 lb. carcass will give 25–30 portions.

For the Winkleton shoot, the spit roast was a fixed spit roast that had a bar on a hinge which clipped into a chain at one end.

METHOD

Cut away the woody parts of the thyme and place in a pestle and mortar, food processor or hand blender, blend lightly then add the garlic and blend again. Now add the salt and blend further then finally add sufficient oil to make a thick paste.

Open out a large clean bin bag onto a clean surface. Lay the carcass on it and, wearing a pair of rubber gloves, smother the whole carcass in the paste. Make sure you cover the outside and inside of the carcass then with some help place a bin bag over the head end and another over the back end. Take some duct tape and seal up the two overlapping bags. You need to do this otherwise you will end up with everything smelling of garlic. Place the carcass in a fridge or, if the winter, you could keep it in a cold garage overnight.

MOUNTING ONTO A FIXED BAR

To mount the carcass, pull the bar out and slide the carcass onto it. Taking some galvanized wire, loop the wire around the end of the shoulders and around the bar, pulling it tight enough to draw them together but allowing the carcass to rotate.

At the other end, do the same with the end of the haunches. Now make three holes along the ribs and thread the wire through these, tying them to hold the carcass in position.

The fire must be lit and should be on its way to burning white hot, that is to say when the logs burn down to nearly the embers. This produces heat without flame.

Swing the carcass back over the fire and, using oven gloves, turn the carcass so that it starts to cook on its side. Allow this to sit for 15-20 mins then turn to the other side, then the belly side and then the back, and so on, until the carcass is cooked. The back should always be last as it is the thinnest part of the carcass and could over-cook most easily.

A probe can be a good way of checking that the meat is cooked. Take the temperature of the thickest part of the haunches: a core temperature of 140°F will be medium rare.

Remove the carcass by cutting away the wire using oven gloves and place the carcass on a cutting board. You need to rest it for 20 mins before carving. Carve the carcass by removing the shoulders, then the haunches and finally the loins.

Venison epigrams (BREAST)

Serves 4 -6

INGREDIENTS

1 medium onion

1 medium carrot

oil for deep frying and frying
vegetables

1 clove of garlic

sprig of thyme

½ bay leaf

2 glasses red wine

2 boned out venison breasts

salt and pepper

5¼ cups venison stock or brown
chicken stock

3 oz. Dijon mustard

about ½ lb. plain flour

2 eggs, lightly beaten

about ½ lb. fresh or panko
breadcrumbs

Epigrams of lamb are good but venison ones are better as they have more flavor. The boned out breasts are cooked slowly until tender in a well-flavored stock with herbs and wine, but they can also be cooked sous vide in wine and herbs for 13 hours overnight at 165°F then pressed. This dish can be eaten as it is or as part of another venison dish.

METHOD

Roughly chop the onion, carrot and garlic. Pour some oil into a deep pan large enough to take venison breasts. Heat the oil and then fry the onion for 5-6 mins. Now add the rest of the vegetables and herbs and cook for another 5-6 mins then add the wine and reduce by half.

Bring the stock to the boil. Place the breasts, on top of the herbs and vegetables. Season and add boiling stock then bring back to the boil slowly.

Reduce the heat and simmer for 2-3 hours or until the meat is tender. When the meat is cooked you should be able to take it in between your finger and thumb and as you pinch your fingers they will go through the meat.

Once the meat is cooked take it out of the stock and allow to cool for 10 mins. Once cooled place one of the breasts on to a sheet of silicone paper on a tray and then place the other breast on top. Cover with another sheet of paper and place a weighted tray on top of both breasts and put in the fridge to cool. The breasts now need to rest and chill overnight.

Remove the paper and carefully place the breasts onto a chopping board. They should have become loosely bound together. Trim and square off the whole breasts then cut into portion sizes. These could be squares, triangles or rounds. Once you have cut them place a wooden toothpick into the center of each portion, this will help you to pick up the portions and will keep the breasts held together when cooking.

Take the pieces holding them by the toothpick and brush them liberally with Dijon mustard then pass lightly through flour tapping off any excess. Next dip in beaten egg and then in breadcrumbs making sure that all surfaces are covered in the breadcrumbs. Do this all while holding onto the toothpick.

Heat the oil to 350°F and carefully lower the breasts into it with the toothpicks standing up. Fry until golden brown then drain on kitchen paper, remove the toothpicks and serve with a venison jus or meat gravy.

Barbecued venison ribs (BREAST)

Serves 5

INGREDIENTS

2 cups tomato ketchup

¾ cup dark soy sauce

1 cup honey

2 Tbsp. smoked paprika

5 cloves of garlic, finely chopped

2 venison breasts prepared for BBQ
(see page 17)

about 1 pint chicken stock

I love barbecued spare ribs. Pork can be very fatty however, so here is a recipe using venison ribs. These can be finished in the oven or on a BBQ and if you go for the latter, be careful they do not burn.

To sous vide, marinate the ribs in a vac pack then double bag them and cook overnight at 165°F. Then chill and baste in the oven to glaze.

METHOD

Place all the ingredients apart from the chicken stock in a bowl and mix well.

Using a pastry brush, paint the BBQ sauce all over the ribs on both sides.

Take a clean large plastic bag and fold out the top of the bag so that you can see the bottom. Place the ribs in the bag and pour over the rest of the marinade. Wash your hands and then unfold the rolled top end of the bag and tie a knot in it.

Leave the ribs to marinate overnight in the fridge.

The following day place the ribs in a heat-proof dish large enough to take them lying down in a single layer.

Tip the remaining marinade into a separate bowl, add the chicken stock, mix well and pour over the ribs, ensuring they are well covered in liquid. Bring the marinade to a boil then transfer to the oven and cook for 1¾ to 2½ hours at 325°F or until the meat is tender.

Remove the ribs from the sauce and allow to cool. Meanwhile strain the sauce and simmer to reduce to a thick coating consistency.

Once the ribs are cold, cut into 3-bone portions then dip or coat with sauce before placing in the oven or on a BBQ to reheat.

Delicious with roasted potato wedges!

Whole braised venison shoulder with navy bean, sweet pepper and tomato cassoulet (SHOULDER)

Serves 4-6

INGREDIENTS

light olive oil

2 medium shoulders of venison, bone-in

salt and pepper

1 large onion

2 cloves garlic

2 red chilis

4 Romano peppers

2 glasses dry white wine

1 28 oz. can of chopped tomatoes

sprig of rosemary

1 qt. game or chicken stock

1 15 oz. can of navy beans

4 fresh plum tomatoes

This is a rustic dish of venison shoulder, slow cooked on the bone. Once cooked, the meat should come away from the bone easily and the sweet flavors of the peppers, tomatoes and beans will complement the meat well.

METHOD

Season and pan fry the shoulders to seal. If they won't fit in your pan, make a cut in each of the muscles so that you can fold them up. Remove from the pan.

Fry the finely diced onion and garlic for 2-3 mins then add the finely chopped chilis and half the coarsely diced peppers. Lower the heat for a further 2-3 mins.

Turn up the heat again and add the wine, reducing down by half.

Then add the chopped tomatoes, the rosemary and the game or chicken stock.

Put the shoulders back in the pan, the liquid should just cover the joints. Bring to a boil.

Place in the oven at 325°F for 2 hours then add the rest of the peppers, the navy beans and the chopped, de-seeded, skinned fresh tomatoes. Return to the oven for another 30 mins at 275°F.

Remove from the oven, take the joints out of the sauce and reduce to the desired consistency.

When you serve the meat, it should come away from the bone easily so that it can be portioned up and served with sauce.

Venison croquettes (SCRAG/NECK)

Serves 4

INGREDIENTS

2.5 quarts venison or dark chicken stock

oil for frying

1 lb. scrag or venison neck

salt and pepper

½ onion, roughly diced

½ clove garlic, cut in half, skin on

1 carrot

2 sticks celery

1 bay leaf

1 sprig of thyme

1 tbsp. tomato purée

2 glasses red wine

4 tbsp. plain flour

2 eggs

½ cup fresh breadcrumbs

These posh croquettes can be served as a dish in their own right or as a starter - or even as part of a venison main course containing other elements. They are a bit of a surprise when you eat them as many people do not expect the filling.

The first part of the dish can take a while to prepare but once the neck is cooked and shredded, it can be frozen and made into the croquettes at a later date. The meat in this recipe could also be cooked sous vide by sealing it in a bag with bay leaf, thyme and red wine then cooking at 165°F overnight. The pulled venison made in this recipe can be used in the same way as pulled pork.

METHOD

Bring the stock to a boil.

Heat a large pan with a little oil.

Take the neck as a whole piece (do not dice), season well and fry in the pan sealing until well browned.

Remove the meat from the pan and add the onion and garlic, frying well for about 7 mins. Add the rest of the vegetables and herbs, and cook further until all the vegetables have a golden brown color.

Add the tomato purée, stir and cook for 2-3 mins then add the red wine. Bring to a boil then reduce by half.

Add the hot stock and the scrag, bring back to boil then cover and simmer gently for 2-3 hours until the meat is very tender and falling apart. During this time remove any scum from the stock with a ladle.

Remove the meat from the stock, strain the stock to remove all the vegetables and then place the stock on the stove to boil and reduce. Meanwhile, while the meat is still hot, pull it apart in strands. You may want to wear rubber gloves to do this.

Once the stock has reduced right down by two-thirds, it will go slightly thicker, like a thick, sticky jus. Pass this again through a fine strainer and add to the meat.

Mix the meat and jus well, allow to cool then place in the fridge to cool.

Remove from the fridge and form the meat into balls or croquette shapes then pass lightly through flour then beaten egg and finally fresh breadcrumbs.

Deep fry the croquettes at 350°F until golden brown. Drain on paper towels then serve.

Herb-rolled venison loin with chanterelle mushrooms (SADDLE & FILLET)

Serves 4

INGREDIENTS

4–⅓ lb. of venison backstrap

salt and pepper

oil for frying

1½ tbsp. butter

2 oz. chanterelle mushrooms, cleaned and cut in half if large

1 cup venison jus *(see page 101)*

2 tbsp. chopped chervil

2 tbsp. chopped flat leaf parsley

2 tbsp. chopped chives

The backstrap is a cut from the loin and is one of the most popular cuts used by chefs. It is boneless and very tender. If you were using beef instead of venison, the cannon would be the equivalent of the beef sirloin.

The venison backstrap requires very little cooking, just searing and roasting in the oven for 7-8 mins, no more, followed by a resting period of 4 mins before carving.

METHOD

Pre-heat the oven to 375°F.

Season the venison backstraps. Heat a small amount of oil in a pan to smoking hot then sear the venison on all sides.

Remove the venison from the pan and place on a baking tray and put in oven for 4 mins. Turn the backstraps over and cook for 4 more mins then remove and allow to rest for 4 mins in a warm place.

While the venison is cooking, melt the butter in the same pan you seared the venison in, add the mushrooms and cook briefly over a high heat.

Add ½ cup of the jus and bring to a boil allowing it to thicken to the consistency of heavy cream then keep warm.

Take the rest of the jus and reduce by half.

Place the chopped herbs in a shallow dish. Holding the cannons at each end with finger and thumb, roll them in the reduced venison jus and then in the herbs. Don't worry about covering the ends. Place each cannon on a piece of plastic wrap and roll it in the plastic wrap twice over and twist the ends. This is to help the herbs to stick to the meat.

Slice then remove plastic wrap and serve with venison jus, mushrooms and potato purée.

Hot-smoked venison loin with Barry's quince jelly

(SADDLE & FILLET)

Serves 4

INGREDIENTS

½ cup sugar

½ cup curing salt

1¾ pint water

1 lb. venison backstrap

QUINCE JELLY

4½ lb. quince

about 2½ cups preserving sugar

micro leaves to garnish

Barry Jones was one of my lecturers when I was at college and now he is one of my colleagues working alongside me here. He has a fantastic quince tree in his garden and from this, every year, he teaches his students how to make beautifully clear quince jelly. Quince jelly is something that has always been known to me as it is served all over Spain, where I spent my holidays with relatives. Quince jelly goes beautifully with smoked meats.

METHOD

Mix the sugar, curing salt and water until dissolved. Place the venison into the solution for 3 hours.

Remove the venison, dry in a cloth then place on a dry cloth on a tray. Put this in the fridge and leave overnight, uncovered, to dry out.

Next day place the venison into the hot smoker once it has heated up. Leave it there for 25-35 mins, turning twice.

The venison should be cooked on the outside but still fairly pink in the middle.

Once cooked, remove the venison from the smoker and allow to cool.

Then wrap the venison tightly in plastic wrap and place in the fridge to become really cold.

METHOD FOR THE QUINCE JELLY

Wash the quince and remove any over-ripe areas. Do not peel.

Chop into ½ inch chunks, place in a heavy-bottomed pan and cover with water. Bring to a boil and simmer until soft, skimming regularly.

Place the fruit and juice in a muslin bag, allow the juice to drain overnight: it will take a long time for the clear juice to drain. Do not squeeze the fruit to extract more juice. Measure the juice—you should have 1½–1¾ cups.

Return the juice to the thick bottomed pan and add preserving sugar at the ratio of ½ cup for every ⅓ cup of juice.

Bring to a boil, continually skimming and using a sugar thermometer until the temperature reaches 220°F. Immediately pour the jam into sterilized jam jars and seal while hot.

Allow jelly to go cold and set.

Serve the sliced venison with the quince jelly and micro leaves to garnish.

Venison carpaccio with gorgonzola and caramelized walnuts (SADDLE & FILLET)

Serves 4

INGREDIENTS

¾ lb. venison tenderloin

vegetable oil

2 tsp. Dijon mustard

1 tbsp. of crushed black peppercorns

¼ c. white sugar

½ c. walnuts

½ c. Gorgonzola piccante

drizzle of reduced balsamic glaze (available from shops)

water cress or micro-herbs to garnish

Maldon salt

Carpaccio is a refreshing starter which, if well done, tastes delicious. Here I use venison filet paired with a fantastic gorgonzola cheese and caramelized walnuts.

METHOD

Season the venison and seal in a very hot pan with a little oil. Allow to cool then take a pastry brush and brush the whole filet with the mustard, then roll it in the crushed peppercorns. Place the venison on a large piece of plastic wrap then roll up tightly and place in the freezer so that it semi-freezes making it easier to slice later.

Place the sugar in a saucepan, add a splash of water then place over the heat and allow the sugar to come to a boil then cook until it starts to turn light golden brown. Watch it carefully in case it burns. Remove from the heat.

Take the walnuts and wash in warm water then dry well. Once dry, drop them one by one into the caramel and carefully roll them so that they are all covered then place them on a sheet of wax paper to cool.

Once the venison is semi-frozen, slice it thinly by hand with a very sharp knife or on a meat slicer, and arrange on the serving plates. Allow about 3 oz. per person.

Sprinkle 2 tbsp. of walnuts and 2 tbsp. crumbled Gorgonzola over each portion of venison then drizzle over the reduced balsamic glaze and garnish with some watercress or micro-herbs and a sprinkle of Maldon salt.

Miso-marinated venison loin with Thai salad

(SADDLE & FILLET)

Serves 4

INGREDIENTS

1½ lb. venison loin

oil for frying

MARINADE

⅓ c. sake

⅓ c. mirin

½ c. sugar

⅓ c. white miso

SALAD

⅔ c. green mango, cut into julienne

⅔ c. green papaya, cut into julienne

⅔ c. carrot, cut into julienne

DRESSING

¼ c. fish sauce

¼ c. lime juice

⅛ c. lemon juice

sugar to taste

Miso paste gives a great flavor to meat. The marinade caramelizes over the meat as it cooks and gives a sweet yet yeasty flavor. This, paired with a refreshing cold Thai salad, works well with the venison.

METHOD

Combine the marinade ingredients in a pan and bring to a boil, simmer for 5 mins then cover and allow to cool.

Place the venison loin in a ceramic, glass or stainless steel container. Pour the cold marinade over the meat and allow to marinate overnight. Turn as needed.

Remove the meat from the dish and scrape off any excess marinade.

Pan fry the meat in some very hot oil, searing on all sides then place on an oven tray.

Re-boil the marinade, allow it to reduce and thicken. Heat the oven to 375°F. Place the meat in the oven and baste occasionally with some of the marinade as it cooks, so that it forms a glaze of caramelized miso over the meat. Cook for 7 mins then rest on one side for 5 mins in a warm place but do not cover.

Combine the ingredients for the salad and dressing in a bowl - the dressing should be salty, sharp and sweet, all at the same time. Toss the salad well. After a few minutes, the salad will soften due to the dressing. Divide it between 4 plates.

Slice the venison and place on the salad. Serve at once.

Smoked venison bacon (SADDLE & FILLET)

Makes about 3 lb. of venison bacon

INGREDIENTS

1 loin of venison with a good layer of fat

1 c. curing salts (available online)

2½ quarts water

A few years ago I started looking at different things I could do with venison apart from cooking it. Charcuterie seemed to be the answer. One of the first things I looked at was the possibility of making venison bacon. I played with this idea until I got what I think is right. You can only make venison bacon from the larger deer species such as red, fallow and sika and you can only make it in the early part of the autumn when the deer are carrying a layer of fat on their backs.

To make the brine we use in the curing process, we use curing salts which are a mixture of salt and nitrate and which can be bought online. These cure the meat and give it its characteristic pink color.

METHOD

Remove the loin (or backstrap) from the long saddle and cut in half. Leave all the fat and trimming on it.

Mix the curing salts with the water to make a brine and mix well so that the salts dissolve.

Submerge the whole loins into the brine and make sure that the meat remains under the water. You may want to place a weighted bowl on top of the meat to help push it under. Also make sure the loins lie flat in the brine.

Allow the loins to remain in the brine for 3 days, turning every day.

After 3 days remove the loins from the brine. If you have a vacuum packer, vac pac the loins and leave for another day to 'equalize' while the salts are absorbed. If not, wrap the meat in plastic wrap and rest it for a day.

Next unpack the loins and if you want to use them unsmoked, place them in the freezer for an hour so that they firm up and are easier to cut with a knife or on a slicer.

To smoke the loins, unpack them from the plastic wrap or remove them from vac pac, pat dry with a clean cloth and then place them on a tray and into the fridge. Leave them uncovered to dry overnight. The following day, cold smoke them for 2 hours. Once smoked, chill down in the freezer as above to make them easier to cut.

Wrap in greaseproof paper or plastic wrap and store in the fridge for 2-3 weeks—or freeze for up to 3 months.

Cold-smoked venison tartare (SADDLE & FILLET)

Serves 4 as a starter

INGREDIENTS

¾ lb. venison fillet

2 tsp. chopped parsley

1 tbsp. gherkins, finely chopped

1 tbsp. fine capers (or large capers, chopped)

1 tbsp. shallots, finely chopped

2 tsp. Worcestershire sauce

a few drops Tabasco

2 free range egg yolks

1 large tsp. Dijon mustard

salt and pepper

fried bread to serve

When preparing a raw meat recipe, we should always look at using the most tender cut available. Tenderloin is that cut and with the tenderloin on most deer being very small, this is a good way of using them.

This a classic tartare recipe with a slight twist in that the venison is cold smoked.

METHOD

Place the trimmed tenderloins into a smoker and cold smoke for 2 hours.

Once smoked, finely dice the fillets (tartare is always finely chopped and never minced) and place in a bowl with all the other ingredients apart from the mustard and egg, mix well, then add mustard and egg yolk then mix well again and season.

Divide the mixture into portions then form into small burger shapes. To serve, place on a piece of fried bread or toast points.

Barbecued butterfly haunch of venison with a rosemary, garlic and olive oil seasoning (HAUNCH)

Serves 6 (depending on size of haunch)

INGREDIENTS

1 venison haunch, boned and butterflied

3 tbsp. chopped fresh rosemary

3 large cloves garlic

about ⅓ c. olive oil

out ⅓ c. Maldon salt

My son Luis loves cooking with me and this is a recipe that allows him to get messy when marinating butterfly haunches. This is a very simple recipe which can be made anywhere, without too much preparation. It tastes wonderful and is similar to my Whole Carcass recipe but here it uses a more manageable joint.

METHOD

Take the haunch and cut the shank off at the joint. Keep this for another day as a shank is too tough to cook on a BBQ. Open bone the thigh by cutting down onto the bone, following it then cutting around it.

Once the bone is out, make a cut either side of where the bone had been to flatten out the venison and make it all one thickness. (Ask your butcher to butterfly the cut for you if you have any problems.)

Place the rosemary, garlic, olive oil and salt into a food processor and blitz to make a paste. Use Maldon salt as it has large flaky crystals which make a good paste without being too 'salty'. Take the paste and rub well in to all the venison on all sides. Place the venison in a plastic bag and pour the rest of the paste over it then tie a knot in the bag and leave for 2 hours or place in the fridge overnight. If it has been in the fridge overnight, take it out and allow to sit for an hour or so before cooking.

Light the BBQ and allow it to get hot. In the case of charcoal, allow to burn until the coals turn white.

Scrape off the marinade from the venison. Place the meat on the BBQ and sear well on both sides, then remove from the BBQ. Take a large square of foil doubled over 4 times with the shiny side out to reflect a little heat. Place this thick foil in the center of the BBQ and then place the venison on top. Close the BBQ lid and allow to cook, turning after 15-20 mins then cook for a further 10-15mins.

Venison should be cooked to rare or medium then allowed to rest for 10 mins before slicing and serving.

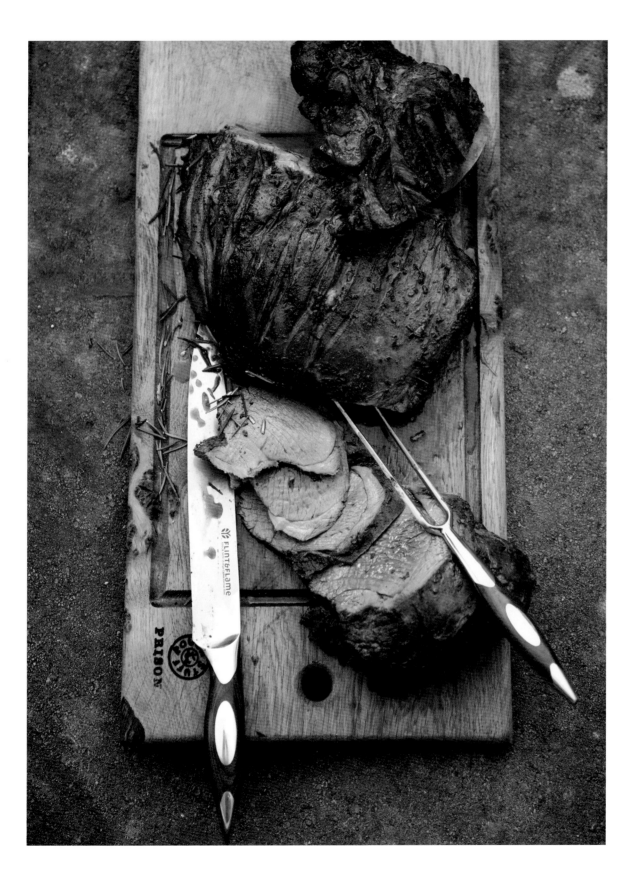

Venison shanks with baby beets and chestnuts

(HAUNCH)

Serves 4

INGREDIENTS

1 c. carrots

1 c. celery

⅔ c. leeks

3 cloves garlic

2 x venison shanks

salt and pepper

1 tbsp. tomato purée

1¾ quarts of dark chicken or venison stock

1 tsp. chopped fresh sage

2 tsp. grain mustard

12 baby beetroot

1 c. cooked chestnuts

2 tbsp. butter

The shank of any animal has lots of flavor since it is a muscle that works hard and contains a lot of sinew which always gives good flavor and substance to any sauce you are cooking. Slow cooked, shank meat will nearly fall off the bone and be a delicious winter warmer.

METHOD

Cut the carrots, celery and leeks into ½-inch dice and roughly chop the garlic.

Season the shanks and fry in a frying pan to give them even color all over.

Place the shanks in an oven-proof dish that has a lid, fry all the diced vegetables in the pan you have used for the venison until colored, then add the tomato purée and cook for another 5-8 mins then add the stock and sage.

Cover the shanks with the stock and diced vegetables. Bring to a boil then cook in the oven at 325°F for 1½-2 hours or until meat is tender. Larger shanks could take slightly longer.

Remove the shanks from the cooking liquid and keep warm and covered so they do not dry out.

Decant the stock into saucepan, passing it through a fine strainer to remove diced vegetables—keep them warm with the shanks. Bring the stock to a boil, stir in the mustard and reduce by half.

Drop the baby beetroots into cold water and bring to a boil until cooked then refresh and peel.

Sauté the chestnuts in about 1 tbsp. of butter to warm through.

Reheat the baby beetroots by plunging into boiling water then drain and toss in 1 tbsp. melted butter.

Place the shanks in a serving dish and cover with hot sauce, then garnish with vegetables, baby beetroots and chestnuts.

Trio of venison steaks (HAUNCH)

Serves 4

INGREDIENTS

Venison steaks are taken from the haunch (or hind leg) muscles: namely, the topside (or top round), silverside and the thick flank. The topside and silverside muscles are solid pieces of meat but the thick flank has a small amount of sinew running through it.

These are all juicy, tender steaks that need only minimal cooking.

SHERRY AND CREAM SAUCE STEAKS

4 x venison haunch or hind leg steaks ⅓ lb. each. from the silverside or topside

salt and pepper

oil

2 tbsp. butter

1 shallot

1 glass of sweet sherry

¼ c. venison or dark chicken stock

¾ c. heavy cream

BLUE CHEESE MELT STEAKS

½ c. heavy cream

1⅓ tbsp. Gorgonzola piccante cheese

4 x venison haunch or hind leg steaks, ⅓ lb. ea. from the silverside or topside

salt and pepper

TERIYAKI GLAZE

¾ c. soy sauce

2 tbsp. honey

4 x venison haunch or hind leg steaks, ⅓ lb. each

¼ c. mirin wine

METHOD FOR SHERRY AND CREAM SAUCE STEAKS

Season the steaks and pan fry in a little oil until cooked to your taste (i.e. rare, medium, well done). Remove the steaks from the pan and allow to rest while you make the sauce. Add the butter to pan. Once melted, add the finely chopped shallots and allow to sweat until soft.

Add the sherry to the shallots and reduce by half, then add the stock and reduce by half. Now add the cream and reduce to a coating consistency.

Season the sauce and serve with the steaks.

METHOD FOR BLUE CHEESE MELT STEAKS

Pour the cream into a saucepan and bring to a simmer then add the cheese. Once the cheese has melted, stir well then pour into a small bowl and allow to cool in the fridge. Season the steaks and pan fry in a little oil until cooked to your taste (i.e. rare, medium, well done). Remove the steaks from the pan and allow to rest. Take the cheese melt out of the fridge.

Place the steak on a heat-proof serving plate and add a spoonful of cheese melt to each one then place under a grill to melt slightly. Serve at once.

METHOD FOR TERIYAKI GLAZE

Mix together the soy sauce, honey and mirin wine in a bowl. Place the steaks in the bowl, making sure they are covered by the marinade. Leave for 2 hours then remove steaks from marinade and pat dry.

Place the marinade in a pan and reduce to a glaze. Pan fry the steak with a little oil until cooked to your taste (i.e. rare, medium, well done).

When the steaks are ready and the glaze is reduced, brush the glaze thoroughly over the steaks then slice with a sharp knife and serve at once.

Delicious with roasted potato wedges, onion rings and mushrooms.

Venison pastrami (HAUNCH)

INGREDIENTS

1 top round roll of venison

1 cup curing salts (easily bought online)

3 quarts water

1⅓ tbsp. olive oil

freshly cracked black pepper

Pastrami is great with salads and in sandwiches. This recipe uses a top round of venison which has been cured and smoked, then cooked slowly, giving a fantastic-tasting pastrami that can be sliced wafer thin. Serve as a starter or to accompany cheese.

Makes approximately 1 lb. of pastrami depending on the size of top round.

METHOD

Remove the top round from the haunch then clean down to the eye of the meat, removing all sinew.

Mix the curing salts with the water to make a brine, and mix well so that the salt dissolves.

Submerge the venison in the brine making sure that the meat remains under the water. You may want to place a weighted bowl on top of the meat to help push it under.

Allow the meat to remain in the brine for 24 hours. Give them a mix every so often.

After 24 hours remove the venison from the brine and pat dry with a clean cloth. Place uncovered on a tray in the fridge overnight to allow the topside to dry off before smoking.

The following day, set up the cold smoker and allow to run for 20 mins then cold smoke the venison for 2 hours. Remove from the smoker and wrap in plastic wrap 4 times over tightly. Tie a knot in each end and poach in simmering water for 35 mins or until cooked all the way through.

[If you are using a vacuum pac and sous vide machine, vac pac the smoked topside and then cook in the sous vide machine at 170°F. for 30 mins].

Once cooked, chill the venison and then roll in olive oil and freshly cracked pepper. Re-wrap in plastic wrap and chill for 1 hour. Slice thinly to serve.

Air-dried venison ham (HAUNCH)

INGREDIENTS

1 haunch (or hind leg) of venison with good fat covering (in this recipe I've used fallow but weights can vary from 5.5 to 18 lb., depending on the species)

7 lb. rock salt (or enough to cover the haunch)

COATING PASTE

1 lb. lard

2 c. black pepper, ground

After a visit to Italy to see the production of Prosciutto di Parma in its home-town, I decided to use this age-old curing technique on a leg of venison.

Firstly I selected a venison haunch with a good amount of fat because this would give me a natural barrier to the meat itself, slowing down the cure take-up in order not to make the meat too salty.

Venison air dried has a flavor all of its own, very unlike Parma or Serrano ham, and it can be cured on or off the bone. November is the best time to start the curing process if you are curing at home and do not have a curing cabinet.

METHOD

Take the haunch or hind leg and remove the aitch bone only, then rub a good amount of salt into the exposed meat, concentrating around the ball joint and the cut surface of the meat, then work your way around the haunch.

Make a bed of salt for the meat to lie on and make sure that all of the meat is coated with salt.

Leave the haunch in this salt for 1 day for every 2 lb. of meat, turning the meat once a day and re-covering the haunch with salt.

At the end of the salting stage, remove from the salt, which will now be very moist - this is normal. Next rinse the ham (salted venison haunch) and pat dry with a clean cloth.

Hang in a fridge for 1 week to allow it to dry off.

After drying the ham, make up a coating paste by mixing the lard and the black pepper: this will stop flies trying to attack the meat (although if you make the ham in the cold months there will be less chance of this). Make sure that you have well covered the exposed, cut area of the ham with the paste, extra special attention again being paid to the ball joint. You can also paste the leg but it is the open face that needs the extra good layer of paste.

Now hang the ham by the achilles tendon in a cool, dark and well-ventilated place for at least 6 months. I hang mine in the roof of my barn.

Slice thinly to serve.

Cold-smoked and roasted hind leg of venison (HAUNCH)

Serves 6–8

INGREDIENTS

1 haunch of venison

Maldon salt

pepper

olive oil

1 large potato

Cold smoking is usually associated with smoked salmon but it is also a good way of giving that same flavor as food cooked on an open fire. There are many different types of woods to choose from when smoking, and bear in mind that just because it is being smoked in apple wood, for example, this does not mean it will taste of apples. Wood such as oak, chicory and mesquite are good all-rounders with a robust flavor but I prefer the fruit woods or alder with venison as it adds a delicate flavor without overpowering the meat.

METHOD

The day before you are going to smoke the haunch of venison, place the joint, untied, on a tray on top of a clean dry cloth and put it in the fridge uncovered overnight to dry the surface of the meat. A dry surface allows the smoke to adhere to the meat more evenly.

The following day set the smoker up as a cold smoker, allowing the chips to begin to burn so that smoke is passing through the unit.

Hang the haunch off a rack within the smoker and allow to smoke for 2½ hours then turn the unit off but leave the haunch in the smoker for another ½ hour. At this point pre-heat the oven.

Remove the haunch from the smoker, season, rub with oil then tie as for roasting.

Take a large potato and slice in half. Place this on a roasting tray and set the haunch on top of the potato - this will stop the bottom of the joint from burning.

Place the haunch in a hot oven at 400°F for about 20 mins so that the joint is seared and colors well. After 20 mins turn the oven down to 350°F and cook for a further 30 mins. I hate giving times per weight of a joint as we all have different ovens. A better way is to take a roasting fork and stick it into the thickest part of the meat: when you withdraw the fork, touch the fork tip to your lips and if it is hot and the juices are pink, the meat is ready if you want a medium rare joint. If the juices are pink but the fork is cold, it needs longer.

Another good way is to invest in a meat thermometer: 125-130°F in the thickest part will be rare, 140-150°F medium rare; 160°F medium and so on. Personally I always cook medium rare as while the meat is resting it just cooks a little more to perfection and if someone in the party would like it more well done, you can always return it to the oven for a few minutes but if you over-cook it, the meat will be dry and tough.

Once the meat comes out of the oven, always rest it for 10 mins before carving.

Venison kidneys turbigo (OFFAL)

Serves 4

INGREDIENTS

16 button or pearl onions

½ c. butter

12 venison kidneys

16 cocktail chipolatas (or mini brats)

24 button mushrooms

2 cloves garlic

¾ c. plain flour

2 tsp. tomato purée

2¾ c. venison or brown chicken stock

4 slices of white bread

parsley to garnish

Turbigo is a dish that I used to serve when I was Commis chef at the House of Commons and it was a firm favourite with the MPs. I prepared this dish for the central buffet where a selection of quick dishes were available, so that MPs could come in and help themselves if they were in a hurry. Turbigo takes its name from a street in Paris which in turn is named after a battle in the town of that name near Milan. This is a dish my father made many times throughout his career as a head Gueridon waiter where it was prepared in front of the guests. Traditionally, this dish is prepared with lamb kidneys but venison kidneys have a fuller flavor and lend themselves well to my version here.

METHOD

Place the button onions in a bowl and pour boiling water over them, allowing them to soak for 5 mins. Remove the onions from the water and carefully peel them, trimming but keeping the outer root intact.

Take half the butter and melt in a pan. When hot, add the button onions and fry gently until they start to go golden brown then remove from the pan.

Next add the kidneys and sauté quickly to sear only, then remove from the pan and place in a bowl. Add a little more butter to the pan then again, when hot, add the cocktail sausages to sear without cooking then remove from the pan and place in a bowl.

Add some more of the butter, and fry the button mushrooms until colored then remove from the pan and place in a bowl.

Add the garlic to the pan and cook for 5 mins. Stir in the flour and cook for a minute then add the tomato purée and cook again for another minute or two.

Next add the hot stock, a little less than 1 cup at a time, stirring well so that there are no lumps and bring to a boil.

Add the onions first and allow to cook for 8-10 mins, or until they are soft.

Now add the kidneys, sausages, and mushrooms and cook for a further 8-10 mins.

Take the slices of bread and cut with a large round cutter then fry in the remaining butter until golden brown.

To serve the turbigo, place a piece of bread in the middle of each plate and spoon some kidney mixture onto it, garnishing with fresh, roughly chopped parsley.

Grilled venison liver and Colcannon potatoes (OFFAL)

Serves 6

INGREDIENTS

2 lb. venison liver

2 cloves garlic

vegetable oil

2 lb. desirée red-skinned potatoes

⅓ c. milk

¾ c. butter

1½ c. cabbage, shredded

5 oz. pancetta

salt and pepper

venison jus to serve *(see page 101)*

Venison liver is said by some to be strong in flavor but I do not find it half as strong as pigs liver. In fact I would go as far as saying that it is only slightly stronger than lambs liver but not in an off-putting way. If you do find it slightly strong for your tastes, then soak it in milk overnight. Liver is very good for you and is rich in iron.

METHOD

Remove the skin from the liver completely then slice at an angle into ¼ to ⅓-inch thick slices. Remove any large arteries.

Thinly slice the garlic and place it in a bowl with a little oil then add the sliced liver to marinade for an hour or two or overnight.

Peel and cut the potatoes in half then boil in plenty of salted water until soft (about 20 mins).

Drain and return to the pan, setting it back over a gentle heat for a couple of minutes allowing the potatoes to dry off. Push the potato through a ricer or mash with a potato masher.

Heat the milk and ½ cup of butter in a pan until the butter has melted then mix into the potato and season.

Blanch the cabbage in boiling salted water for 6 mins then dunk in cold water and drain.

Fry the pancetta in some oil then drain on paper towels.

Add the cabbage and pancetta to the mash.

Heat a griddle pan until smoking hot.

Remove the liver from the marinade oil and wipe off excess oil. Season. Cook on one side for 3 mins then the other side for the same length of time.

Once cooked, remove from the pan and leave to rest.

Meanwhile melt the remaining butter in a frying pan until frothing then add the mash, allowing it to color slightly before folding over. This will allow all the crispy bits of potatoes on the outside to mix into the mash. Keep turning until the mash is heated through.

Serve the liver with this colcannon and a little venison jus.

Braised venison hearts filled with pork sausage

(OFFAL)

Serves 2 to 4, depending on the species of venison

INGREDIENTS

2 venison hearts

1 onion, finely chopped

1 sprig of thyme

3½ tbsp. butter

4 slices of back bacon

½ lb. pork sausage meat (amount will depend on size of heart)

salt and pepper

1 tsp. freshly chopped sage

2 carrots, cut in small dice

2 sticks of celery, cut in small dice

¾ c. plain flour

1⅔ quarts of venison or dark chicken stock

2 large tsp. Dijon mustard

Hearts are rich in iron and, unlike most other offal, have a meaty texture. Venison hearts can be braised as in this recipe but they can also be thinly sliced and pan fried. The size of the animal dictates the number of portions you will get from a heart.

METHOD

Take the hearts and remove the arteries at the top by cutting a slit straight across the heart. Next using a small knife cut away all the strands inside the hearts, hollowing it out ready to take the stuffing.

Take half the onion and thyme and sweat it gently in a little butter without coloring it for 5 mins. When the onion is soft, allow to cool.

Take the bacon and cut off the thin streaky part, reserving the eye of the bacon. Chop the streaky bacon.

Place the sausage meat, chopped sage and chopped bacon in a bowl. Add the cooled onion to the sausage meat. Mix well and season generously.

Take the hollowed-out hearts and at the tip make a cross-shaped cut about ½-inch deep. Fill each heart with the sausage mixture right up to the top, pressing it down as you go so that there are no air pockets.

Take the bacon eye slices and lay 2 of them over the top of the hole you have been stuffing in each heart to completely cover the stuffing.

Set heart, bacon-side down on a piece of butchers' string, then take both ends of string up to the top of the heart to the cross cut you made earlier.

Cross the strings over each other and pull down onto the heart so that the string slips into one of the cuts at the tip but no tighter. Now turn the string 90 degrees and allow it to slip into the other part of the cross cut, then take the ends down underneath the bacon, tying a knot to hold everything in place. Repeat with the second heart.

Melt the rest of the butter in a deep oven-proof pan.

Season the hearts and sear them well on all sides in the butter, over a medium heat. Remove the hearts and keep to one side but keep the pan on the heat and reuse it to cook the rest of the onions for 4-5 mins then add the rest of the vegetables and cook for a further 4-5 mins. Add the flour and allow to cook for another 5 mins, stirring.

Bring the stock to a boil and add a third to the vegetable mixture, stirring well to break up any lumps. Once the mixture thickens like a paste, add another third of the stock, again stirring well. Stir in the rest of the stock to make a thin sauce. Don't worry if the sauce looks too thin because it will reduce in the oven during cooking so it is better to be slightly on the thin side at this point.

Bring the sauce to a boil. Carefully place the hearts into the sauce then cover with foil and cook in the oven at 325°F for 2 hours or until the hearts are tender.

Once cooked, remove the hearts and the vegetables from the sauce. Cover and keep warm then allow the sauce to boil and reduce to the consistency of double cream. Stir in the mustard and a small knob of butter, whisking lightly.

Untie the hearts, slice and serve on a bed of vegetables with some sauce.

Venison and black pudding skinless sausages

(MINCE & DICE)

Makes 8 sausages

INGREDIENTS

¼ c. pearl barley

1¼ lb. venison, coarsely minced

1¾ oz. venison fat or pork belly fat minced (if using venison fat, freeze then mince it)

3 lb. black pudding (or blood sausage), cut in less than ¼-inch dice

good sprig of fresh thyme

salt and pepper

oil to fry

These are great skinless sausages that can be made into any shape you like. You can even make them into a salami shape which you can poach, slice and then pan fry to give crispy edges.

METHOD

Put the pearl barley in a pan and cover with cold salted water then bring to a boil and simmer 20-30 minutes or until soft.

Rinse the pearl barley in cold water then drain.

Put the venison, fat, black pudding and pearl barley in a bowl.

Strip the leaves from the thyme and chop, then add to the bowl.

Mix all the ingredients well and season generously.

Divide the mixture into 8 balls and roll each into a sausage shape. Lay out a piece of plastic wrap double the length of a sausage and roll the sausage tightly in it.

Twist each end and tie a knot in it so that it holds the meat firmly. Wrap the rest in the same way.

Poach the sausages in simmering water for 10 mins then lift out and cut the end of the plastic wrap with a pair of scissors. Push the sausages out of the plastic wrap.

Heat the oil and fry the sausages until browned then serve with onion gravy and mash.

Venison and porcini mushroom pudding (MINCE & DICE)

Serves 4-6

INGREDIENTS

vegetable oil

2 lb. shoulder of venison, diced

⅓ c. plain flour

⅓ c. dried porcini mushrooms

3½ tbsp. butter

1 onion

1 heaped teaspoon tomato purée

1¾ c. venison or brown chicken stock - *see page 100*

FOR THE PASTRY

3 c. plus 1 tbsp. plain flour

1 tbsp. & 1 tsp. baking powder

pinch of salt

1⅔ c. suet

8¾ oz. water

This meat and mushroom pudding is the essence of comfort food as it tastes as comforting as it looks. The filling can be made the day before and allowed to cool and then the pudding filled the following day. A great dish to cook ahead and it creates a real spectacle when you cut into it at the table.

METHOD

Heat a little oil in a large pan. Season the cubes of venison and dust in flour. In a separate pan, add the porcini mushrooms to the stock and bring to boil, then simmer for 10 mins.

Take half the venison, add to the pan with the hot oil searing the meat well so that it colors on all sides. Remove from the pan and sear the rest of the meat. It is important to get good color on the meat because this is what will determine the color of your sauce. Set the seared venison to one side.

Melt the butter in the same pan and add the finely chopped onion. Sweat for 3 mins then add the venison and the tomato purée and cook for another 2-3 mins. Stir in the hot stock with the porcini mushrooms so that all the flour dissolves and creates a sauce. Bring to a boil, then simmer gently for 1½ hours until meat is cooked, then allow to cool.

FOR THE PASTRY—Sift the flour, baking powder and salt. Mix in the suet then make a well in the center. Add water and mix lightly to make a soft paste that comes away from the edge of the bowl. Remove about a quarter of the dough and keep covered to one side. This will be your lid. Roll out the remaining dough to a circle about 16 inches diameter. Butter a 2 quart (8-inch) pudding basin and line it with pastry, allowing the pastry to be slightly higher than the top of the basin.

Roll out the lid dough into a circle about 8 inches diameter for the lid. Fill the lined pudding basin with the cold meat and mushroom mixture. Set the lid over the pie mixture so it sits snugly and covers it completely. Brush the edges with cold water and fold any excess pastry over the edge of the bowl to seal the lid.

Cut a circular piece of greaseproof paper 3 times as large as the top of the pudding, butter the paper and form a pleat in the middle of it, then place on top of the pudding, folding the excess paper over the edge and then tie a piece of string around it to keep it in place.

To cook, put a folded cloth into a saucepan of boiling water and then stand the basin on it, so that the water comes three-quarters of the way up the basin (the cloth will stop the bottom of the puddings burning). Place a lid on the saucepan and cook for 45 mins, then remove from the water. Discard the paper lid then turn out the pudding onto a warmed serving plate.

Venison tea with parmesan and filet dumplings

(MINCE & DICE)

Serves 4

INGREDIENTS

CONSOMMÉ

1 c. each of carrot, celery, onion

2 egg whites

1 lb. (neck or shank) venison with
no fat, minced

salt and pepper

2⅔ quarts double-strength venison
stock (⅔ q. cold and
2 quarts hot)—*see page 100*

DUMPLINGS

⅓ lb. venison filet

⅓ c. parmesan

salt and pepper

1 tbsp. chopped chives

GARNISH

⅓ c. carrot and turnip

This 'tea' is a strong venison consommé with some small but tasty dumplings. The stock needs to be a double-strength stock: this means that you make a stock and then you make another stock but instead of using water, you use the stock you have already made. This will strengthen your main stock and give you a stronger flavor.

In times gone by, these soups were served at the end of Balls just before the guests went home. The rich, strong flavor of these consommés (known as beef teas when made with beef stock) fortified them for the carriage rides. This is my version made with venison.

METHOD

Roughly chop all the vegetables apart from the onion then pulse 4 or 5 times in a food processor. Very finely chop the onion by hand and add to the vegetables.

Whisk the egg whites until just starting to froth then add the minced venison and vegetables. Mix well and season with salt and pepper.

Add the cold stock to the venison and vegetables. Mix well (this mixture is called a clarification) and allow to stand in fridge for 20 mins.

Pour the hot stock into a large pan and add the clarification, mixing well. Stir occasionally until it comes to boil then DO NOT STIR any more but turn down the heat and simmer very gently for 1 hour 45 mins.

While the soup is cooking, take the finely chopped venison filet and place in a bowl with the finely grated parmesan and chopped chives and lightly season. Mix together well, then roll into even, marble-sized balls.

Take the carrot and turnip for garnish and dice very finely and evenly then blanch for a few seconds in some boiling salted water. Drain and place in ice-cold water.

Once the soup is cooked, carefully push the raft of floating vegetables and mince to one side and carefully ladle out from below the crystal-clear liquid (consommé). Pass the consommé through a fine strainer or muslin cloth into another saucepan. If the soup is a little greasy, gently lay a piece of paper towel on its surface for two seconds to absorb the grease.

Fry the venison balls quickly in a little oil to lightly color only. Remove from pan and place on paper towels to drain.

Warm the serving bowls and gently warm the soup but do not boil. Place some of the vegetable garnish into serving bowls, add the hot soup, drop in the venison dumplings and serve.

Winter venison stew (MINCE & DICE)

Serves 4

INGREDIENTS

vegetable oil

2 lb. neck or shoulder of venison, diced

salt and pepper

⅓ c. plain flour

1 onion

2 cloves garlic

2 tsp. tomato purée

1⅓ quarts venison or dark chicken stock

4 large carrots

2 turnips

2 small swedes/rutabagas

8 baby onions

2 tbsp. butter

All the flavors of winter are in this classic dish but it will fail to deliver if the meat is served dry or tough. The secret is to use neck or shoulder, well seared on all sides to ensure you lock in the moisture and flavor and slow cook to keep it tender.

METHOD

Heat a little oil in a large low-sided pan to smoking point (very hot). Season and dust all the venison in the flour.

Add half the venison to the pan and sear, making sure it colors well (this makes the color of the sauce), then remove. Reheat the pan and repeat with the rest of the venison. Remove from the pan.

Add a little more oil and sweat the finely chopped onion and garlic for 3 mins. Add the venison and the tomato purée and cook for another 2-3 min. Stir in the remaining flour then add the boiling stock slowly to create a sauce. Bring the stew to a simmer then cook over a low heat for 1hour 30 mins or until the meat is tender.

Meanwhile peel and shape the vegetables all to the same size apart from the onions which should be peeled whole and the roots trimmed. Cook them all in a little stock until tender, then set aside.

Remove the meat from the sauce and keep warm in a covered bowl.

Bring the sauce to a boil and adjust the consistency by adding more stock if too thick or reducing if too thin. Stir in a couple of pads of butter to give the sauce a rich shine. Place the meat back into sauce, garnish with the vegetables and serve.

Venison and pasta roulade (Nidi di Rondine)

(MINCE & DICE)

Serves 4

INGREDIENTS

FOR CHEESE SAUCE

1 ¾ c. milk

½ onion

1 bay leaf

2 cloves

4 tbsp. butter

⅓ c. plain flour

pinch nutmeg

FOR THE MEAT SAUCE

light olive oil

2 lb. ground venison

1 onion, finely chopped

2 cloves of garlic, very finely chopped

1 large carrot, finely chopped

2 sticks of celery, finely chopped

2 tsp. tomato purée

1 sprig thyme

1 tsp. chopped oregano

1 bay leaf

⅓ c. plain flour

1 28 oz. can of chopped tomatoes

1 quart venison stock or dark chicken stock

FOR THE ROULADES

4 fresh lasagna sheets

8 slices of good quality ham

2 c. parmesan cheese, grated

½ lb. mozzarella cheese, thinly sliced

I love this recipe because it is very different yet uses familiar ingredients. Its proper name is Nidi di Rondine or to translate, Swallows' Nests. This is a dish from northern Italy although there are many variations in the way it can be interpreted. It comes from the Italian mother of a good friend of mine and as soon as I tasted it, I wanted to know the recipe which she finally divulged to me over a family dinner. It is a recipe I have used over the years in many of the places I have worked, tweaking it here and there, but it's as good today as the day Mama Ispani made it. This is a venison version of this great dish.

METHOD

Pour the milk for the sauce into a saucepan, add the ½ onion, bay leaf, pinch of nutmeg, and cloves. Bring to a boil and then turn off the heat and keep warm. In a separate pan, bring the stock to a boil and keep warm.

Melt the butter in a saucepan, add the flour and mix to form a roux. Cook for 2 mins then remove from the heat and allow to cool slightly. Discard the onion, bay leaf and cloves from the milk then place the roux back over the heat and stir in a third of the milk (a little more than 1/2 c.), mixing well until smooth then add another third, stirring until smooth and then add the final third. Turn the heat down and allow to simmer for 20 mins then leave to go cold.

Pour a little oil into a large saucepan and when hot, add half the mince and fry until cooked then remove. Add some more oil to the pan, reheat and fry the rest of the meat and again remove from the pan.

In the same pan cook the onion and garlic in a little oil without coloring. After 5 mins add the carrot and celery and cook until softened. Add the meat, stir well then add tomato purée, herbs and cook for 4 mins. Add the flour and stir well, then stir in the chopped tomatoes and cook for a further 5 mins. Add the hot stock and bring to boil.

Simmer over a gentle heat for at least an hour and a half. If it reduces a lot and becomes too thick, add some more stock. Adjust the seasoning.

While the meat sauce is cooking, take a large wide saucepan and in salted boiling water poach the lasagna sheets for 2-3 mins then remove and chill briefly in cold water. Lay the pasta onto a clean dry cloth and pat it dry, take some of the now cold béchamel sauce and spread it over the sheet of pasta, then lay 2 ham slices on the sauce and finally sprinkle with parmesan and overlay the slices of mozzarella. Keep some of the béchamel to finish the dish.

Starting at the short end, roll the pasta sheet up like a cigar then wrap in a piece of plastic wrap. Do this with each of the pasta sheets then place in the freezer for 30 mins to firm up.

Remove from the freezer and trim the ends to give a flat end, remove the plastic wrap then cut the roulade into 4. Take an oven dish and place a little of the béchamel on the bottom of the dish, then set the roulade pieces in the dish with the ends facing up. Ladle the meat sauce over the middle of the roulades then add a ladle of béchamel over this.

Finally, sprinkle the rest of the cheese on and bake for 35 mins at 350°F or until cheese has melted.

Serve at once.

Moroccan-style venison tagine (MINCE & DICE)

Serves 4

INGREDIENTS

light olive oil

2 lb. venison shoulder, diced

1 onion

3 cloves of garlic

2 tsp. ground cumin

1 tsp. turmeric

2 tsp. garam masala

1 tsp. ground coriander

1½ tsp. harissa paste

1 tbsp. tomato purée

1 14 oz. can chopped plum tomatoes

1 quart white game or chicken stock

½ c. sultanas or golden raisins

½ c. dried apricots

¼ c. almonds, whole, blanched

fresh coriander

1½ c. couscous

salt and pepper

fresh coriander to garnish

This dish was inspired by the flavors of Moroccan cookery where sweet and savory are combined to produce a melting pot of fruit and spice flavors. Serve with couscous or rice to make a hearty meal.

METHOD

Heat some oil in a large shallow pan. When hot, add half the venison and sear on all sides then remove from pan. Repeat with the rest of the meat and remove from pan.

Next, finely chop the onion and garlic and in the same pan used for the meat, gently heat some more oil to sweat the onion and garlic for 4-5 mins – don't let it color.

Lower the heat and add the dry spices and harissa paste to the onions and garlic, allowing the oil to warm the spices and release their flavors. Return the meat to the pan and stir well. Add the tomato purée and cook for another 5 mins on a low heat. Add the chopped tomatoes, bring to a boil stirring, then add the hot stock and again stir back to a boil then turn the heat down to a simmer for 1 hour 30 mins or until the meat is tender. Ten mins before serving, add the sultanas, apricots and almonds.

Add 1 c. of boiling water to the couscous, season, stir well then allow to stand for 10 mins then garnish with the chopped coriander.

Venison kofta kebab (MINCE & DICE)

Serves 4

INGREDIENTS

KOFTAS

1 lb. minced venison shoulder,
or scrag

2 tbsp. chopped fresh coriander

2 tsp. turmeric

2 tsp. chili powder

4 tsp. ground cumin

2 tsp. ground coriander

2 cloves garlic

YOGHURT SAUCE

1 tbsp. chopped fresh coriander

¾ c. natural yogurt

1 tsp. honey

RED ONION SALAD

2 tbsp. olive oil

2 tsp. white wine vinegar

1 tsp. sugar

1 red onion, finely chopped

½ tbsp. fresh unchopped coriander
leaves

Venison lends itself well to spices so here is a recipe that can help you use mince from the shoulder or neck. Make sure that it is well diced and all sinew is removed. Once mixed, do not handle too much as this will toughen the meat. You can make this in advance and freeze it, defrosting and molding onto sticks or making into burgers when you are ready.

METHOD

Place the venison into a large bowl and add all the spices, 2 tablespoons of the chopped fresh coriander and the finely chopped garlic.

Mix well then cover and place in fridge overnight.

The following day take some wooden skewers and soak them in water - this will help them not to burn when the koftas are cooking.

Take the mixture and divide into even balls then thread one or two onto each of your skewers.

Oil your hand and shape the meat into a sausage shape of equal thickness along the skewer.

The koftas can be cooked on a griddle, in a pan or on a BBQ, cooking equally on each side. Do not over-cook or they will become dry.

While the koftas are cooking, take the 1 tbsp. chopped fresh coriander for the sauce and add this to the yogurt. Then add the honey and mix well.

Place 2 tbsp. of oil in a bowl, add the white wine vinegar and the sugar, whisk with a fork to emulsify the dressing then toss the red onion and the remaining unchopped coriander leaves in the dressing.

Serve the koftas with the red onion salad and the yoghurt sauce.

Venison lasagna (MINCE & DICE)

Serves 6

INGREDIENTS

FOR THE MEAT SAUCE

1 quart venison stock or dark chicken stock

light olive oil

2 lb. ground venison

1 onion, finely chopped

2 cloves of garlic, very finely chopped

1 large carrot, finely chopped

2 sticks of celery, finely chopped

2 tsp. tomato purée

1 sprig thyme

1 tsp. chopped oregano

1 bay leaf

⅓ c. plain flour

1 can (28 oz.) of chopped tomatoes

CHEESE SAUCE

1¾ c. milk

½ onion

1 bay leaf

2 cloves

4 tbsp. butter

⅓ c. plain flour

¾ c. cheddar cheese, grated

¼ c. parmesan, grated

1 lb. fresh or dried pasta sheets

Lasagna is an Italian classic normally made with ground beef but ground venison is a great alternative, as it is low in fat and full of flavor. My wife Charlotte loves this recipe and I often make it at home to freeze and eat at a later date.

METHOD

In a saucepan bring the venison stock to the boil and keep warm.

Place a little oil in a large saucepan. When hot, fry half the ground venison until cooked then remove from the pan. Add some more oil to the pan, reheat and fry the rest of the meat and again remove from pan.

In the same pan cook the onion and garlic in a little oil without coloring. After 5 mins add the carrot and celery and fry for 4-5 mins, then add the meat, stir well, add the tomato purée and herbs and cook for 4 mins. Stir in the flour well, add the chopped tomatoes and cook for a further 5 mins. Add the hot stock and bring to a boil.

Cook over a gentle heat for at least an hour and a half. If it becomes too thick, add some more stock. Correct seasoning and allow to cool before using.

Put the milk, ½ onion, bay leaf and cloves in a saucepan. Bring to a boil then turn off and keep warm. In a separate saucepan melt the butter, stir in the flour and mix to form a roux. Cook for about 2 mins then pull off the heat and allow to cool slightly. Remove the onion, bay leaf and cloves from the milk then place the roux back on the stove over a gentle heat. Stir a third of the milk into the roux, mixing well until smooth, then add another third, stirring again until smooth and then the final third. Turn the heat very low and allow to cook for 30 mins then add ¼ cup of the cheddar cheese and all the Parmesan to the sauce, stir well, then allow to cool.

Once the meat and cheese sauces have cooled down, take a deep oven-proof dish and start by spooning a little of the cheese sauce into the dish, then place some of the pasta sheets onto the sauce. Now add a layer of meat sauce to coat the pasta then cover with more pasta and then sauce. Continue this layering until you are ½-inch below the lip of the dish then finish with a layer of cheese sauce and sprinkle the last of the cheddar cheese on top.

Pre-heat oven at 375°F then place the lasagna onto a baking tray to catch any drips and cook for 1 hour, checking that the center is cooked and hot before serving.

Stalker's breakfast (BREAST, SHOULDER, SADDLE & FILLET)

Serves 4

INGREDIENTS

8 venison sausages *(see below)*

16 slices of smoked venison bacon

4 pheasant eggs, fried

CONFIT TOMATOES

2 tomatoes

4 thin slices of garlic

sprig of thyme

Maldon (or sea) salt

virgin olive oil

100% VENISON SAUSAGES

2 lb. venison, coarsely ground
(shoulder or breast)

½ lb. + venison fat, coarsely ground

¼ lb. crushed ice

4 oz. dried breadcrumbs

salt and pepper

½ lb. natural sausage casings

On a cold winter's morning after you have been out stalking, there is nothing like a hearty breakfast to help you along with the day. Here is the ultimate hunter's breakfast with venison sausages, venison bacon, a pheasant egg (when in season, and if not, a duck egg) and confit tomato. The fat in the sausages is venison fat which I collect from fatty venison carcasses, dice and then freeze. (Some cooks may wish to substitute pork or beef fat for venison fat.)

METHOD

FOR THE CONFIT TOMATOES

Pre heat oven to 200°F.

Cut the tomatoes in half and place on a baking tray then set a slice of garlic on each one and a sprinkle of thyme and salt. Drizzle a little of the oil over the tomatoes and place in the low oven and cook for 2 hours or until soft. Once cooked, they can be cooled down and eaten cold or warmed up.

METHOD FOR VENISON SAUSAGES

Place the ground venison and venison fat in a bowl, mix in the crushed ice and breadcrumbs then season well. Make a small patty and fry this sample to taste for seasoning—add more if needed.

Place the meat into a sausage machine and force into the natural casing then make into sausage shapes by twisting the skin at 6 to 7-inch intervals. Do not over-fill the skins.

Pan fry or grill.

SMOKED VENISON BACON—*see page 52*

Smoked venison and pork chorizo (BREAST OR SHOULDER)

Makes 20 to 30 sausages

INGREDIENTS

6½ lb. venison (shoulder or breast)

4½ lb. pork belly

6 cloves garlic

¼ lb. curing salts

1 tbsp. crushed black peppercorns

1¾ c. smoked paprika

⅔ lb. crushed ice

1 lb. + natural sausage skins

Venison will take spice well. These chorizos are great cooked just as they are, or as part of a major dish like a cassoulet. I have on occasion made these chorizos by adding only venison fat instead of pork fat/ belly thereby making 100% venison sausages. Venison has very little fat but in autumn some deer carry more fat on their backs than usual. This fat can be collected, diced and frozen then minced frozen so that it will go through the mincer more easily and used in the same way as pork fat/belly to give you a chorizo sausage that anyone, including those with religious dietary restrictions, can eat.

METHOD

These sausages can be cooked and eaten as soon as they are made or they can be hot smoked.

Grind the venison and pork belly through a coarse die (make sure the meat is well chilled as it will go through the mincer more easily).

Chop the garlic then, using the flat side of the knife or a pestle and mortar, crush the garlic to a paste.

Mix the two meats together well.

Then add, a little at a time, the salts, pepper, paprika, garlic and crushed ice and mix again well. Keep doing this until all the ingredients are mixed.

Place the meat mixture into a sausage machine and force into casings then link into sausages.

To hot smoke, place in a smoker and cook for 25-30 mins and serve at once.

To cold smoke, once in the skins hang and rest overnight to dry the sausages, then cold smoke for 2 hours then they can be cooked in the usual way.

Venison or game stock

INGREDIENTS

5 lb. venison bones

2 lb. + venison trim (any off-cuts from the carcass)

4 large carrots, roughly chopped

1 large onion, roughly chopped

2 sticks celery, roughly chopped

oil

1 bay leaf

sprig of thyme, roughly chopped

water

A good stock is the base of all sauces and care should be taken when making one. The stock needs any scum or impurities that float to the surface skimmed off and removed. It is also important that the stock is not boiled hard for a long period. It should be brought to boil then turned down to a simmer. This way, it will remain clean and clear.

METHOD

Fry or roast venison bones and off-cuts so that they get a good brown color.

Fry or roast all vegetables with a little oil to reach a good brown color.

Place bones, vegetables and herbs in a large saucepan and cover the top of the bones by at least 2 inches of cold water.

Bring to a boil skimming all the time. Then simmer very gently for 4-5 hours, skimming from time to time.

Strain and discard the solids. The stock can be chilled and any fat that solidifies on top can be removed. Then it is ready to use or freeze.

DOUBLE-STRENGTH STOCK

A double-strength stock is one that has been refreshed by re-cooking with more bones. To make a double-strength stock, follow the recipe for making stock but instead of using water to cover the bones, use the stock you have already made. Look after the stock as it simmers, skim regularly and do not boil.

Double strength stocks are great for soups where a full-bodied stock is required.

Venison or game jus

INGREDIENTS

2 lb.+ venison/game trimmings, cut into a small dice

oil to fry

2 large carrots, finely diced

1 large onion, finely diced

1 stick celery, finely diced

3 cloves garlic, not peeled, just cut in half

2 tsp. tomato purée

½ bottle red wine

sprig of fresh thyme

about 1⅓ gallons venison or game stock *(see page 100)*

salt and pepper

A venison or game jus is a reduced fortified stock, that is to say, a good stock that has been enriched with meat trimmings and then allowed to reduce so that the natural gelatine in the meat acts as a natural thickening. A jus has no flour or any other thickener in the sauce. It can be quite strong and should be used sparingly as it can overpower the meat.

METHOD

Fry the venison trimmings in a little oil to give a good color. Do a bit at a time. Remove from pan and keep to one side.

Fry the diced vegetables and garlic in same pan with a little more oil, again to give good color.

Add the meat trimmings to the vegetables and then add tomato purée. Fry for 2-3 mins.

Add wine and thyme and simmer to reduce by half.

Add stock, season and reduce by two-thirds.

Strain through a fine strainer.

The jus should be the consistency of single cream. If you require a thicker consistency reduce further but be careful not to burn it. This would be known as a glace. The jus and glace can also be frozen and used whenever needed.

Jus

Glace

A trophy whitetail buck.
Photo Credit: Getty Images

CHAMPIONS OF VENISON

Over many years in the industry, I have worked with lots of talented individuals, some of whom have become great friends. A number of them, as professional chefs, have attended some of my one-day game seminars and I am honored when they say they have found them something of an education, an eye-opener.

I have had the pleasure of taking several of these chefs out stalking with me, not necessarily to harvest deer but sometimes just to see deer in the wild or in some of the deer parks. This gives them a better understanding of the whole business of stalking and the provenance of the venison they cook. This understanding is something all chefs strive for as it gives us a deep-rooted respect and passion for the product. Most chefs love cooking with venison and will use it whenever their budgets or menus allow.

Here are 13 well-known professional chefs who enjoy using venison in a variety of very different ways and who are excited by the prospect of cooking a wild, natural meat.

My thanks to them all: good friends and true masters of their craft.

With grateful thanks to my friends for their support and the time they gave creating these fantastic recipes. Ben Tish, Chris Galvin, Steven Poole, Mike Robinson, Peter Gordon, Tom Kerridge, Phil Vickery, Brett Graham, Cesar Garcia, Jun Tanaka, Jeff Galvin, Rachel Green & Cyrus Todiwala

Venison carpaccio with dandelion, marcona almonds, lardo & quince

Serves 4 as a starter

BEN TISH
THE SALT YARD GROUP

José is one of the most enthusiastic, passionate chefs I know (don't get him started on venison!) Seriously though, what he doesn't know about game and venison isn't worth knowing. I will never forget a demonstration at Westminster College hosted by José in which he butchered a whole red deer in front of a bunch of chefs and foodies. It was captivating to watch someone with so much skill and precision, and with such passion for his subject!

We love venison at the Salt Yard group and it's always on the menu in season. I like the versatility of it, as well as the obvious things such as flavor. It has become very popular now due to its reputation for being so healthy. I love doing venison carpaccios and tartares but I also like using the more unusual parts, like the liver. The pronounced flavors of the meat work well with our big, gutsy style.

INGREDIENTS

½ lb. venison haunch (or top round), well trimmed

glass red wine

1 sprig thyme

1 clove garlic

3 juniper berries

3 peppercorns

olive oil for cooking

sea salt and pepper

16 salted marcona almonds

1 head of dandelion, trimmed and washed

1 oz. Italian lardo (cured, seasoned pork fat)

½ c. extra virgin olive oil

¼ c. moscatel vinegar

2 tsp. quince membrillo (jelly)

METHOD

Marinade the venison in the wine with the aromats and leave to cure for at least 4 hours. Remove the venison and pat dry, season well with salt and pepper and rub with olive oil.

Heat a grill pan over a high heat and grill the venison on all sides very quickly. Ensure all sides are seared properly and the inside is still rare. Rest the meat for a few minutes then wrap very tightly in plastic wrap to firm the shape ready for slicing. Transfer to a fridge for at least 1 hour.

Melt the quince membrillo in the vinegar over a very low heat in a small pan. Whisk in the olive oil and reserve.

Slice the lardo very finely into strips and reserve.

TO PLATE

Remove the venison from the fridge and with the cling film intact, slice the venison very thinly. Remove all the cling film and then divide the slices between four serving plates. Season the meat and then spoon over some of the quince dressing. Scatter over the nuts, pick over some dandelion and then drape over some slices of lardo. Serve at room temperature.

Maple-cured venison, sage & pumpkin

Serves 2 as a main course

**TOM KERRIDGE
HAND AND FLOWERS**

Having had a lengthy conversation with José while we were both doing cookery demonstrations at Chatsworth House, I'm very proud to include a venison recipe here that helps lift that full-on flavor of venison to another level. Venison is a wonderful lean meat in plentiful supply and is surprisingly good all year round.

INGREDIENTS

½ lb. center-loin of venison

FOR THE MARINADE

¼ c. maple syrup

2 tsp. cider vinegar

¼ c. chicken stock

⅓ c. venison jus *(see page 101)*

FOR THE CARAMELIZED PUMPKIN PURÉE

¼ small crown prince pumpkin

⅓ c. demerara sugar

splash of malt vinegar

pinch of cinnamon

½ c. butter

FOR THE VENISON SEASONING

6 sage leaves (fried until crispy must be green)

venison glaze

Cornish sea salt

chopped Douglas fir pine

FOR THE VENISON RAGU

¾ lb. venison shoulder, ground

½ c. rich venison sauce

1 tsp. cracked black pepper

1 tsp. toasted cumin

FOR THE BACON ROAST SQUASH

1 x butternut squash peeled and seeds removed

¼ lb. bacon fat

Tbsp. pumpkin seeds toasted

Tbsp. pecan nuts toasted

Tsp. chopped chives

METHOD

Mix the chicken stock, vinegar and maple syrup together, pour over the venison fillets and marinate for 3 hours. Remove the venison and put the marinade into a pan with the venison jus and reduce to a glaze. Retain for use when plating up. Plastic wrap the venison nice and tight and cook at 135°F for 45 min in a fan oven until the core reaches 135°F, then turn the oven down to 125°F.

While the venison cooks, dice the pumpkin and lay in a tray with the sugar, vinegar, cinnamon and butter and bake until soft then remove it from the oven, strain off the juices and reduce to a glaze.

Put the pumpkin and glaze into a blender and puree until smooth and glossy, then plastic wrap and keep warm.

Cut the squash lengthways into 8-10 wedges. Take two equal-sized wedges, lay in a small tray and pour over the rendered bacon fat, cover with tin foil and bake until just cooked for about 30 min, basting halfway through. Leave to cool.

FOR THE RAGU

Bake the ground venison until dark, drain off and then add this to a saucepan with the cumin, pepper and sauce, cook out until the venison is super tasty and tender, season and keep warm.

In a non-stick frying pan heat a little oil and add the squash and fry until lightly colored and even. Remove from the pan, season with sea salt, the pecans, pumpkin seeds and chopped chives.

Remove the venison from the oven. Heat a frying pan, add a little oil, season the loin and then lay in the pan with a little knob of butter just to color. Remove and rest. Fry the sage then season it and drain on paper to cool. Slice the venison into 6 equal slices and season with the pine and salt and serve with the squash and sage.

TO PLATE

Plate the purée and then the squash, add a spoon full of the ragu and lay the loin on top. Finish with a little venison glaze and the fried sage.

Deer meatloaf with onions, smoked pancetta & pot roasted beets

Serves 6–8

PHIL VICKERY
CELEBRITY CHEF ON
THIS MORNING (ITV)

Venison and other game are a vital part of country life. Low in fat, largely organic feeders, and in abundance—these all seem pretty good reasons to eat more.

José's love of the countryside and passion for teaching and cooking is very similar to my own. I have attended his superb game classes and have admired his thirst for learning. There's nobody better to write a book on venison and all that goes with it.

INGREDIENTS

⅔ lb. smoked pancetta cubes

1 tbsp. vegetable oil

3 onions, finely chopped

2 cloves garlic, finely chopped

1 lb. ground venison

½ lb. good-quality sausage meat

½ lb. ground partridge, pheasant or duck

2 tsp. dried oregano

1 tsp. ground cinnamon

1 tsp. dried chili flakes

1 tsp. allspice

3 slices white bread, no crusts, made into breadcrumbs

1 medium egg

4 tbsp. roughly-chopped parsley

ground black pepper

METHOD

Pre-heat the oven to 375°F.

Heat the oil in a pan and add the pancetta, cook until nicely browned. Remove and drain well. Add the onions and garlic and cook for 5 mins to color lightly.

Meanwhile, place the meats into a large bowl and mix in oregano, cinnamon, chili flakes and allspice. Add the breadcrumbs, egg, parsley and pepper, season with black pepper and mix well. When the onions and garlic are ready, add to the meat mixture and mix again,

then spoon into a 2lb non-stick loaf tin and flatten well.

Top with the sautéed pancetta cubes. Cover with 2 layers oiled foil and secure around the tin.

Place onto baking tray (to catch any fat that may run) and cook in a pre-heated oven for about 1 hour, or until the juices run clear. Remove from the oven and cool.

Press lightly: place a thick piece of cardboard on top of the foil, then balance a couple of tins of baked beans or similar on top. Chill well in fridge, best overnight.

Remove from the tin, slice and wrap in clean foil or cling film. Keep in the fridge until ready to go.

This can be re-warmed, sliced, in a microwave if required.

ROASTED BEETS (*4 servings*)

4 medium red beetroots

4 medium yellow beetroots

4 medium red-ringed beetroots

1 head fresh garlic

DRESSING

3 tbsp. sherry vinegar

2 tbsp. Dijon mustard

5 tbsp. extra virgin olive oil

4 tbsp. chopped fresh basil

salt & pepper

Pre-heat the oven to 425°F.
Place the beets in a tray; add 1 head of garlic sliced in half. Cover tightly with foil and bake 45-50 mins, or until tender.

Once cooked, remove the tray from the oven. Then (I recommend using rubber gloves) remove the foil and peel away the skin, which will rub off easily. Remove the cooked garlic cloves from the bulb, roughly paste and add to the dressing when finished.

Cut beets into thin wedges and place in a bowl. In a separate bowl, whisk the vinegar, mustard and oil.

Add salt, pepper, fresh basil and pasted garlic. Mix well.

Serve warm with the loaf and creamy mashed potatoes.

TO PLATE

Serve with roasted beets and creamy mashed potatoes.

Agro dolce slow-cooked wild fallow venison shoulder, with Barbaresco Nebbiolo wine & bitter chocolate

Serves 6-8

STEVEN POOLE
GRUBWORKZ

I was the chairman of the Quality Food Awards at a foodie event, and José was a newly-invited judge. I happened to mention that at the time Phil Vickery and I had a food business together and that Phil was equally passionate about feathered and furred game, cookery of course, a fondness from pigs to partridge, and that they should meet. Later I met photographer Steve Lee and was utterly blown away by his skills in food photography, technical and art direction and by his thirst for wonderful food and the odd glass or two of Guinness.

I think it's José's holistic understanding of game which has helped me gain a better and broader view on game and wildlife conservation in this country. It's easy to stand on your soap box and shout about this and that, but through José, going out stalking together, learning to be at one with the landscape, his fascinating game demonstrations, watching Steve capture spectacular photographic images – all this has really galvanised my understanding and changed my perceptions on game management.

I appreciate now just how important it is to ensure that we can all enjoy the exciting and often rare glimpse of wildlife so that our children can grow up in a world full of healthy, diverse and natural wildlife species.

So for that reason we should thank people like José, Steve and all the other thousands of unsung people in this country who work so hard to maintain the existence of such wonders of nature that we all take for granted.

INGREDIENTS

4½ lb. boned venison shoulder joint (but knuckle-bone in)

⅜ c. plain flour

3 c. Barbaresco Nebbiolo wine

3 c. venison/chicken stock

½ c. virgin olive oil

2⅓ c. carrot, finely diced

1½ c. celery stalk, finely diced

½ c. shallots finely diced

⅔ c. leeks sliced

2 tbsp. garlic cloves, finely chopped

1½ tbsp. butter, unsalted

½ lb. smoked pancetta bacon lardons

10 oz. portobello mushrooms cut into large pieces

1 tbsp. juniper berries finely chopped

1 tbsp. rock salt

1 tsp. black pepper coarse milled

½ oz. thyme sprigs

1 oz. sage leaves roughly chopped

⅛ c. cane sugar unrefined

⅓ c. aged balsamic vinegar

⅞ c. Valrhona Abinao Bitter Chocolate (85% cocoa solids)

¼ c. raisins

1¼ c. sour cherries semi-dried

⅓ c. pine nuts toasted

½ c. hazelnuts, toasted, coarsely chopped (use half for topping garnish)

4 tbsp. flat leaf parsley coarsely chopped

METHOD

Start by pouring yourself a glass of the amazing Barbaresco Nebbiolo red wine.

Now put the boned (knuckle in) and strung shoulder on a board and season with rock salt and coarse

112

black pepper, lightly coat with flour.

Heat half the olive oil in a large deep-sided casserole on high. Brown the venison, turning after about 5 mins. Transfer to a plate.

To the pan, add the remaining olive oil and butter, heat, then add the carrot, celery, shallots, leek and garlic. Sauté, stirring well, for 5 min or until the vegetables are soft.

Have another slurp of wine; it's lovely isn't it?

Next add the smoked pancetta bacon pieces, chopped juniper berries, fresh thyme, portobello mushrooms and sage, cook for a further 3-4 min or until browned.

Return venison to pan and add the cane sugar, stock, balsamic vinegar, three-quarters of the sour cherries, and red wine and bring to a boil, then reduce to low heat and cook, covered, for 2 hours or until the venison is tender.

Add the broken pieces of Valrhona Abinao chocolate into the remaining stock/juice mixture and bring to a simmer, stirring occasionally, for 4-5 min or until the chocolate is melted and sauce has slightly thickened.

TO PLATE

Place the venison on a board or large plate and garnish with remaining sour cherries, raisins, chopped toasted hazelnuts, pinenuts and chopped parsley before serving.

113

Roast venison with red leaves & vegetables, smoked bone marrow & rhubarb

Serves 4 as a main course

BRETT GRAHAM
THE LEDBURY

Venison for us is the most fascinating English ingredient. We use Chinese water deer, muntjac, roe deer, sika and fallow. They all vary in size, taste and texture during different times of the year. We appreciate and only use wild deer from different regions of England. I met José at the Game Fair at Blenheim Palace. José does superb work at Westminster College in both teaching and inspiring the young students there to cook with venison and other English wild game.

INGREDIENTS

4 loins of venison (approx ⅓ lb. each) at room temp

1 large red beetroot—baked in foil and cut in slices (save trimmings)

8 red endives—broken into leaves and caramelized

8 x red radicchio leaves —separated and cooked in a touch of dry sherry and orange juice

beetroot purée (blend beetroot trimmings with a little red wine vinegar)

1 stick of Yorkshire forced rhubarb, poached and sliced

½ c. venison sauce made by roasting bones

dried blackcurrant powder

4 slices of beef bone marrow cold-smoked over hay

4 baby onions, cut in half and peeled. Cooked alongside the rhubarb

METHOD

Sear the venison in a warm pan and cook in oven at 300°F until pink. Warm your tray of beetroot, rhubarb and onions in the oven. Then caramelize radicchio and endive and keep warm. Warm bone marrow until soft and pour a little bit into the venison sauce.

TO PLATE

On warm plate, place down some beetroot purée then endive, radicchio, beetroot, rhubarb and onions. Place on the venison loin with a slice of bone marrow. Finish with the sauce and a sprinkling of dried blackcurrant powder.

Deer tenderloin filet, pine, roast garlic, honey alioli & ceps

Serves 4 as a main course

CESAR GARCIA
IBERICA

From the first day I met José, I was struck by the passion and dedication he has for his work, students and everything food-related, but also by his special love affair with all things related to deer and falconry. Enjoying a drink with José or watching him in the field, is to learn something new about this world, as I experienced first-hand when I went stalking with him: an unforgettable day in the heart of the countryside, at one with nature's wild food larder. Venison lives in the wild and I bring together two elements of nature in my recipe here: the pine tree that gives the deer food and shelter and the aromatic herbs in which the noble roe deer lies, and which infuse its light flavor.

Deer fillet, cut in half lengthways

AROMATS

1 orange peel

2 mint leaves per slice of fillet

2 large sage leaves torn into pieces

1 thyme sprig per filet piece

4 leaves rosemary per fillet

4 thinly-sliced cloves garlic

black pepper

Place the filet slices on a tray and top with all the small pieces of the herbs and orange peel, followed by the garlic. Season with black pepper.

Leave for 24 hours in the fridge.

PINE OIL

1¾ c. extra virgin olive oil

8 sprigs of pine

Place the pine sprigs in warm oil and allow to infuse for 40 min.

ROAST GARLIC & HONEY ALIOLI

8 garlic cloves

1 egg yolk

1 tbsp. honey

¾ c. sunflower oil

½ tsp. sherry vinegar

pinch of salt

Bake garlic in the oven at 325°F for 15-20 min.

Peel garlic, place in a measuring cup with the egg, salt, sherry vinegar, honey and ¼ of the sunflower oil.

Blend together, adding rest of the oil very gradually.

SALAD

3 cups watercress

2 cups ceps or porcini mushrooms

1½ tbsp. toasted pinenuts

2 tsp. sherry vinegar

1 tbsp. & 1 tsp. extra virgin olive oil

Clean the mushrooms, cut into slices then pan fry.

Make a vinaigrette using the sherry vinegar and olive oil.

Dress the watercress in a bowl with the pinenuts and the mushromms.

⅓ c. venison jus - *see page 101*

FINISH

Put the meat on a skewer, season with salt and pan fry to your taste using the pine oil and serve on the salad garnish with the alioli and the venison jus.

To complete the authenticity of the dish, the meat can be served with pine sprigs used as skewers, giving a rustic touch that is full of flavor.

Venison haunch cooked in a spiced salt crust

Serves 2 as a main course

JUN TANAKA
CELEBRITY CHEF

We should all eat more venison! It has so many good qualities: it's higher in protein than beef, pork, chicken and lamb, but it's lower in calories, cholesterol and fat. Venison is always free range and thoroughly sustainable. You would think that taste would have to be sacrificed for all these benefits but actually, it's the opposite: it's packed with flavor!

Most importantly, don't be intimidated when you're cooking venison. Treat it in a similar manner to beef, but remember, it's leaner so it is easier to overcook.

I was introduced to José and the work they had done on this book through photographer Steve Lee. And when I saw Steve's vivid photos and the delicious recipes, I instantly knew that José is a chef who is truly passionate about game. Needless to say, when I was asked to contribute a recipe, I jumped at the chance!

INGREDIENTS

Venison haunch (hind leg) separated into individual muscles (trim the sinew)Take 1 piece weighing ⅔–1 lb.

FOR THE SALT CRUST

¾ c. plus 2 tbsp. coarse sea salt

1⅔ c. plain flour (plus extra for dusting)

1 egg white

⅓ c. water

1 tbsp. ground black pepper

4 tbsp. ground star anis

2 tsp. ground cinnamon

3 tbsp. ground juniper berries

FOR CARAMELIZED CHICORY

2 red chicory (cut in quarters lengthways)

1 orange (juiced)

1 lemon (juiced)

Few leaves of mint cut into very fine strips

1¾ tbsp. butter

2 tbsp. sugar

¾ c. fresh chicken stock (not stock cube)

½ c. plus 2 tbsp. walnuts (toasted)

METHOD

To make the salt crust, add the salt, spices (keep a little to one side), egg white and water into a large bowl. Slowly add the flour and knead until you form a smooth dough. Cover with plastic wrap and rest for 1 hour.

Brown the venison all over in a very hot pan for 1 min. Take out and sprinkle with the reserved spices. Roll the salt crust to ⅓-inch thickness. Place the venison in the middle of the sheet, cut the sheet into a cross shape, fold the edges over the venison until it is completely enclosed. Make a small hole in the top and cook in a pre-heated oven at 435°F for 15 min. To check how it's cooked, insert a metal skewer into the hole and leave for 10 seconds. Place the skewer on the back of your hand and it should feel warm. Remove from the oven and rest for 5 min.

To cook the chicory, melt the butter in a frying pan, add the chicory, season, add the sugar and cook for 2 min. Pour in the juice and chicken stock and simmer for 6 min. Finish with chopped mint.

TO PLATE

Place the chicory on a plate, crack open the salt crust, wipe the venison with paper towels, slice and place next to the chicory. Add the toasted walnuts and spoon the juice from the chicory over the venison.

Slow-cooked venison with quince & chestnuts

Serves 4 as a main course

JEFF GALVIN
GALVIN RESTAURANTS

Venison always appears on our menus during the autumn and winter months. For me it is one of our best native wild meats. I love to use some of the less fashionable cuts such as shoulder and neck of venison, which we slow cook. They have so much flavor and provide superb value.

Many years ago I went to Westminster College to attend José's game seminar and watched him break down three carcasses of different species of venison. He's one of the world's leading chefs on the subject of game and how fantastic it is that he is teaching the next generation of UK chefs about it with such enthusiasm.

INGREDIENTS

3½ lb. shoulder of venison, sinew removed

2 c. red wine

1 c. port

2 large carrots, cut into 2-inch pieces

2 onions, each cut in half

1 stick celery, chopped

3 garlic cloves, chopped

3 juniper berries

3 white peppercorns

½ cinnamon stick

1 sprig of thyme

2 bay leaves

1 sprig of rosemary

⅓ c. olive oil

¾ c. plain flour, seasoned

1 tbsp. tomato purée

2 quarts brown chicken stock

⅔ c. trompette (or black chanterelle) mushrooms

2 tsp. clarified butter

12 chestnuts, roasted and skinned

sea salt and freshly ground white pepper

chopped fresh parsley, to garnish

FOR THE QUINCE

½ c. super fine sugar

¾ c. water

1 lemon

1 quince

METHOD

Put the venison, wine, port, vegetables, garlic and spices together in a non-metallic dish. Tie the thyme, bay and rosemary together with string and add. Cover and leave in fridge for 24 hours. Drain the meat, vegetables, spices and herbs, reserving the meat, vegetables and marinating liquor separately. Pour half the olive oil into a heavy-based oven-proof pan and heat until almost smoking, then add the reserved vegetables and cook until caramelized. Dust the venison in seasoned flour, add a little more olive oil to the pan and sear the meat all over. Stir in the tomato purée and cook briefly with the meat. Remove the meat to a colander to drain, carefully pour the red wine and port from the marinade into the pan and reduce a little, then add the chicken stock and return to a boil. Skim off excess fat or scum, salt to taste then return the venison to the pan. Cover with a lid, transfer it to a preheated oven 230°F and cook for 2½ –3 hours or until venison is tender.

Meanwhile, cook the quince. Bring the sugar and water to a boil, stirring for 2 mins, then remove from the heat. Juice the lemon into a small bowl. Peel the quince and place in the lemon juice, tossing to prevent discoloration.

Cut the quince into 12 wedges, de-seeded and cored. Add with lemon juice to the sugar syrup and bring to a boil, then cover the mixture with a cartouche (a circle of greaseproof paper) and simmer the quince for 6 min or until tender, then set aside.

Remove the venison from the oven, leave to cool then divide into 4 pieces. If the sauce is too thin, boil until slightly reduced and thickened, then pass through a fine sieve back over the meat.

Just before serving, gently reheat meat and sauce together. Heat the clarified butter in a pan, add the trompette mushrooms and toss for 1 min, then season and drain on paper towels before keeping warm. Reheat the quince if necessary and then remove from the syrup with a slotted spoon. Put the chestnuts in an oven preheated to 375°F for 1 min to heat through.

TO SERVE

Put the venison on 4 serving plates, scatter over the mushrooms, chestnuts and quince. Spoon over the sauce and sprinkle with parsley. We often serve this with buttery celeriac purée.

Venison with smoked potato purée, pickled red cabbage, chocolate & watercress

Serves 6 as a main course

CHRIS GALVIN
GALVIN RESTAURANTS

We think venison is a perfect choice of meat for a number of reasons. All the chefs in our restaurants know an ingredient's provenance, which with venison is easy to trace. And we know they have fed naturally and lived happily and healthily. Of course flavor is paramount and the layers and depths of flavor that are revealed with braising, grilling or roasting make it one of the most interesting meats available. Venison lends itself to many accompaniments and is a healthy choice.

A complete understanding of cooking venison properly takes a lot of study in the kitchen and the countryside. Having the advice of an expert like José, with his lifetime of experience in this field, assists anyone's mastery of venison cookery.

INGREDIENTS

FOR THE RED CABBAGE

1 small red cabbage

4 juniper berries

1 star anise

1 bay leaf

6 tbsp. unsalted butter

2 tbsp. demerara sugar

¾ c. red wine

¾ c. port

⅔ c. Cabernet Sauvignon vinegar or other good quality red wine vinegar

sea salt and freshly ground white pepper

FOR THE SHOULDER OF VENISON

2 onions

2 carrots

2 sticks celery

¾ lb. venison shoulder, cut into ⅓-inch dice

1 sprig of thyme

1 bay leaf

2 garlic cloves, chopped

10 black peppercorns

10 juniper berries

2 c. red wine

olive oil, for cooking

1¾ c. brown chicken stock

1¾ c. chicken stock

FOR THE RED WINE AND CHOCOLATE SAUCE

1–2 tablespoons olive oil

trimmings from the loin of venison

1 shallot, sliced

1 carrot, chopped

1 garlic clove, crushed

1 sprig of thyme

10 black peppercorns

5 juniper berries

1 star anise

3½ tbsp. Cabernet Sauvignon vinegar or any good quality red wine vinegar

1¼ c. red wine

1¼ c. brown chicken stock

3 tbsp. bitter chocolate (minimum 70% cocoa solids), finely chopped

FOR THE SMOKED POTATO PURÉE

1½ lb. Charlotte or other waxy new potatoes

½ c. milk

½ c. double cream

1 free-range egg yolk

⅔ c. chilled unsalted butter, diced

FOR THE LOIN OF VENISON

6 portions of boned and trimmed venison loin (about 4 oz. each)—keep the trimmings

1 tablespoon olive oil

2 tbsp. unsalted butter

12 sprigs of watercress, to garnish

METHOD

Cut the cabbage into quarters, core, then shred. Smash the juniper berries and tie them with the star anise and bay leaf in a muslin bag. Melt the butter in a large casserole over a medium heat until foaming, add the cabbage and cook gently for 2–3 min, stirring continuously. Add the muslin bag of spices and the sugar, cook for a further 2 min, then add the wine, port and vinegar. Bring to a boil, cover with a lid and place in an oven preheated to 275°F. Cook for 2–3 hours, stirring every 30 min until soft and glazed. Season with salt and leave to cool, then transfer to an airtight container, cover and refrigerate until needed, up to 4 days.

For the shoulder of venison, chop all the vegetables roughly into 1-inch pieces, then put in a large bowl with the venison shoulder, herbs, garlic, peppercorns and juniper berries. Pour over the wine, then cover and refrigerate overnight. Next day, drain the venison, reserving the wine and vegetables separately. Pat the shoulder dry with a clean cloth. Place a large, deep casserole over a medium heat, add a little olive oil and heat thoroughly. Season the venison with salt and pepper and sear in the hot pan on all sides until browned. Remove the venison and drain on a tray lined with paper towels.

Wipe any excess fat from the pan then heat it again, adding a little more oil, then the reserved vegetables and cook until browned, stirring continuously. Add the venison and the reserved wine and bring to a boil, skimming off any scum. Add the 2 stocks and bring to a boil again, then cover with a disc of greaseproof paper and the lid and place in an oven preheated to 275°F. Cook for 3–3½ hours or until the meat is tender. Remove from the oven and leave to cool for 1 hour.

Drain the mixture through a fine sieve, reserving the meat mixture and cooking liquor separately. Return the cooking liquor to the casserole and boil until it has reduced to a thick and sticky sauce. Flake the meat, then add it to the reduced sauce and season. Grate the carrot pieces and stir them into the meat and sauce (discard the rest of the vegetables). Cover and set aside.

For the red wine and chocolate sauce, heat the olive oil in a large pan over a high heat, then add the venison trimmings and cook until browned all over. Add the shallot, carrot, garlic and thyme and continue to cook until softened. Crush the peppercorns, juniper berries and star anise together and sprinkle 2 pinches into the pan (keep the rest for later), then add the vinegar and cook until it has reduced to a syrup. Make sure all the meat trimmings are coated in the syrup, then add the wine and boil until reduced by half. Add the stock, bring to a boil, then simmer for 30 minutes, skimming off any scum.

Pass this sauce through a fine sieve into a clean pan. Whisk in the chocolate and season to taste—add more crushed spice mixture if required, then simmer for 2–3 min. Strain the sauce again and set aside.

For the smoked potato purée, either wrap the potatoes in foil and bake on an outdoor barbecue over charcoal, or burn the skins with a blowtorch to give a smoky flavor, then bake them on a bed of salt in a hot oven until tender. While they are still hot (wear rubber gloves), peel the potatoes with a small knife, then purée them in a potato ricer or push them through a fine drum sieve to get a very smooth consistency. Bring the milk and cream to a boil in a saucepan. Place the potato flesh in a separate pan over a low heat and pour in half the milk and cream mixture, beating until smooth. Add the rest of the milk and cream and beat until smooth, then add the egg yolk and beat well. Slowly add the diced cold butter, beating all the time to emulsify. Once all the butter has been added, season with salt and pepper, then spoon the mixture into a piping bag fitted with a medium plain nozzle.

Season the venison loin with salt and pepper. Heat a large, heavy-based frying pan over a high heat, add the olive oil, then sear the venison portions, turning every 2 min, until browned on all sides.

123

Reduce the heat to low and add the butter. Cook for 2–3 min, turning the venison every minute in the foaming butter. Remove the venison to a warmed plate and leave to rest in a warm place for 6–8 min before serving.

TO PLATE

Re-heat the red cabbage gently in a pan. Divide the shoulder of venison between 6 deep oven-proof bowls, about 3½-inch in diameter, pipe the smoked potato on top and brown under a hot grill. Put the red cabbage on 6 serving plates. Slice each portion of venison loin diagonally in half, season with a little sea salt and place on top of the cabbage. Reheat the sauce, add a few pomegranate seeds, then spoon it over the venison loin. Garnish with the watercress.

Serve the venison shoulder and smoked potato separately.

British venison cutlets with herb & mustard crust & autumn berry compote

Serves 4 as a main course

RACHEL GREEN
FARMER CHEF AND GAME BIRD

I feel honored that José is including my venison recipe in his book and more so knowing that I am one of the few female chefs to contribute.

I have known José for a number of years - our paths often cross at food festivals due to our mutual love of game and the countryside. We both have a passion for the countryside and shooting. I have huge respect for José and value our friendship, both on a personal and professional level. It always makes me smile when I hear that we are demonstrating cookery at the same events.

José is well-respected in the food industry and by his colleagues and students at Westminster College. I take my chef's hat off to you, José, for keeping the creative juices flowing. You're a top bloke!

INGREDIENTS

8 French-trimmed thick venison cutlets

sea salt and black pepper

4 tbsp. rapeseed oil

2 tbsp. butter

FOR THE HERB CRUST

2 tsp. Dijon mustard

3 tbsp. softened unsalted butter

¾ c. fresh white breadcrumbs

handful finely-chopped parsley leaves

2 tbsp. fresh rosemary leaves, chopped

1 tbsp. fresh thyme leaves, chopped

sea salt and black pepper

FOR THE NEW POTATOES

¾ lb. baby new potatoes

2 sprigs fresh thyme

a few cloves garlic, peeled and crushed

2 tbsp. rapeseed oil

2 tbsp. butter

FOR THE AUTUMN BERRY COMPOTE

1 lb. autumn berries to include blackberries, mulberries and myrtle berries

6 crushed juniper berries

1 star anise (optional)

zest and juice of one small orange

2 tbsp. runny English honey

METHOD

Preheat oven to 400°F

For the potatoes, cut the potatoes in half lengthways and par boil for 8 minutes, drain and cool slightly. Put the potatoes into a bowl and toss with the oil, thyme, garlic, sea salt and black pepper. In a roasting tray, melt the butter. Roast the potatoes for approximately 30-40 minutes, until golden brown.

For the venison cutlets, while the potatoes are roasting, season the cutlets generously with sea salt and black pepper.

Mix the mustard and softened butter to form a paste. Mix the breadcrumbs and parsley, rosemary and thyme together. Spread the butter paste over each side of the cutlets; try to keep the bones clean. Then press each cutlet in the breadcrumb mixture, coating each side well.

Heat a pan with 4 tablespoons of rapeseed oil and 2 tbsp. of butter. When the oil and butter is hot, sear the venison cutlets on both sides until the surface is golden brown. No longer than 1 min on each side.

Place the venison in the oven on top of the roast potatoes and cook for 3-5 minutes until the meat is rare.

Remove the venison cutlets and potatoes from the oven and rest for 3-5 minutes.

FOR THE AUTUMN BERRY COMPOTE

Put all the ingredients into a pan and simmer gently for 2 min or until the fruit releases its juice slightly.

TO PLATE

On a large warm platter place the potatoes in the middle of the platter and lay the venison on top.

Serve with the autumn compote in a small cruet.

Venison steaks with mushroom, horseradish and mustard sauce

Serves 4 as a main course

PETER GORDON
THE PROVIDORES & TAPA ROOM

In New Zealand, my home country, we have been farming venison for decades, as well as shooting it in the bush as José does, and I love the flavor of it. It's lean, healthy, tasty and more versatile than many people realize. It handles spice well, and likes the gameiness of mushrooms and herbs. In the following recipe you can use fresh porcini and trompette de la mort when in season, and you can even add a little smoked paprika or ground smoked chipotle chili to the sauce as it is simmering.

I first met José at Westminster Kingsway College when I was judging the NZ-UK Link Foundation Culinary Challenge and he mentioned that he loved hunting game. I attended, and sent my own chefs to the game classes he runs, where I saw my first muntjac deer and learned the difference between the species. I am a chef who not only loves to cook venison, I also really like to eat it, so I have always enjoyed discussing it with José.

INGREDIENTS

4 x 6 oz. venison steaks (½–¾-inch thick)

1 tbsp. coarsely ground black pepper

2 tsp. flaky salt

2 tbsp. olive oil

1 large red onion, peeled, halved and thinly sliced

¼ lb. chestnut or button mushrooms, thinly sliced

¾ c. double cream

1 tbsp. horseradish sauce

2 tsp. wholegrain mustard

½ teacup snipped chives or thinly sliced spring onions

1 handful watercress or pea shoots

METHOD

Pat the venison dry and rub with salt and pepper on each side. Leave to sit 10 min, then brush with 1 tbsp. of oil.

Heat a frying pan until smoking-hot over medium high heat. Add the steaks and press down firmly, cooking for 1½ min each side. At this point they will be rare: cook longer as desired but venison is a lean meat so over-cooking will dry it out. Remove the steaks, cover loosely and keep in a warm place while you finish the sauce (don't wash the pan as it contains lovely flavors).

Using the same pan, reduce the heat and drizzle in the remaining oil. Add the onion and sauté until softened, stirring frequently to prevent it sticking to the pan.

Add the mushrooms and cook until wilted. Add the cream and bring to a boil.

Reduce the sauce by one third then mix in the horseradish and mustard, along with any juices which have run from the venison. Add seasoning to taste and stir in the chives or spring onions.

TO SERVE

Place venison steaks on warmed plates and spoon the sauce around them and garnish with the watercress or pea shoots. Serve with a side bowl of mashed potatoes or roast sweet potato chunks and steamed greens.

Royal venison sheek kavaab

Serves 4 as a main course

CYRUS TODIWALA
CAFÉ SPICE

My earliest experience with venison was when I was not even ten years old, and I was intrigued by the flurry of activity in the kitchen as a whole deer carcass was skinned, cleaned, washed and divided amongst the huntsmen.

We ate it as kavaabs and everyone relished it. Dad always told me that venison is great for spicing and making kavaabs of different types and to this day I do very little else with venison - it is amazing how versatile this meat is, and how adaptable to spicing.

In India we have several classic dishes revolving around game. In Rajasthan a famous liqueur was made from musk deer and was a favorite with the Maharajas. We also make a very popular venison pickle which originally hails from Rajasthan - we have altered some of

the processes to suit the modern kitchen. Venison has infinite possibilities.

José Souto, the master of game, has been known to me for years now since I was first associated with Westminster Kingsway College. José has boundless energy when it comes to talking and showcasing his favorite topic, namely game, and within that, venison takes pride of place. There are very few people in the UK more knowledgeable about the culinary qualities of venison, nor who are more keen on educating the wider public about its adaptability for regular cooking. This book fulfills that purpose for him and is by far the most influential book on this wonderful animal and the fabulous meat it produces.

INGREDIENTS

1 lb. venison shoulder, cubed

¾ oz. fresh coriander, including stalks

¾ oz. fresh mint, including stalks

1 inch piece of fresh ginger, cut coarsely

6-8 garlic cloves

1 tsp. garam masala powder

1 tsp. ground cumin

1 tsp. ground coriander

1 large fresh green chilli

½ tsp. ground red chili

½ tsp. turmeric powder

1 tsp. lime juice

salt to taste

Once the mince is ready, mix in:

6 dates (seeded and finely chopped)

6 apricots (organic unbleached, chopped)

1 heaped tbsp. walnuts, chopped

METHOD

Clean the meat well removing all sinews and gristle. Do not discard any fat. Cut the meat into small pieces and then mince the meat and the fat. Add all the other ingredients listed and stir well. Salt to taste then mix in the dates, apricots and walnuts. Cover and chill in the refrigerator.

To make the kavaabs you either need a tandoor or you can grill them over a barbecue. Ensure that whatever you are cooking over is lit or heated to a high degree before you start forming the mince over the skewers. Thick square ones are the best. Use round ones if necessary— but they must be thick.

Take a two-inch ball of the mince in one hand and a skewer in the other. Make the ball as smooth as possible by tossing it like a ball in your hand. Now press the ball at roughly the middle of the skewer and press around so that the mince is now covering all round that part of the skewer. Now apply a little oil or water to the palm that you use for the mince and by gently pressing the meat, make it in the form of a sausage on the skewer. This does take a bit of practice and you may find that initially the mince falls off the skewer. But if you form a ring between your forefinger and thumb and use the rest of the fingers to guide the mince, you will be fine. The pressure has to be gently applied and the mince pushed upwards so that it thins itself out over the skewer. Ideally the size of the sausage should be around one inch or a bit less in diameter.

Once you have achieved this you can suspend the skewer on a small tray so that the skewer rests over the two opposite sides and allows the minced area to remain in the hollow of the tray. Complete this with all the skewers.

When you are ready, place them in a similar way, either over the barbecue or in the tandoor as recommended by the manufacturer.

Do not over-cook as this makes the kavaab dry and chewy - it should ideally feel spongy but juicy. About 2 minutes on each side should be about right.

TO PLATE

Serve with fresh green chutney and an onion based salad.

Or roll in a chappati or a flour tortilla filled with salad and sliced onion.

Deer T-bone, cutlets and kromeski with pomme purée, buttered beans & old-school peppercorn sauce

Serves 2 as a main course

MIKE ROBINSON
THE POT KILN

This little recipe is a classic at The Pot Kiln and uses some of the best cuts of the fallow deer - my favorite! Peppercorn sauce really works with fallow, complementing the meat perfectly.

I have known José for seven or eight years—it's impossible to work in the field of game cookery and not know him! We both share an all-consuming passion for the British countryside, and the sporting traditions which have given us such a fabulous amount of consumable and sustainable wildlife. We are both avid deerstalkers and deer managers, and seem to spend more and more time together.

I have always been a bit in awe of José's ability to inspire a young generation of chefs with his work at Westminster College, and I have huge respect for what he does.

He's not only a good rifle shot, but I've seen out in the field how much he loves and respects deer - the sign, in my eyes, of a properly good, respectful and knowledgeable countryman.

___

INGREDIENTS

POT KILN MARINADE

6 cloves garlic

big bunch of thyme

big handful of rosemary

small handful of parsley

zest of a lemon

½ c. extra virgin olive oil

20 black peppercorns

2 fallow T-bones

2 fallow cutlets

FOR THE VENISON IN THE KROMESKI

1¼ lb. shoulder/neck of venison

2 glasses red wine

½ c. water

1 stick celery

1 carrot roughly chopped

½ onion

1 sprig rosemary

FOR THE KROMESKI

4 large shallots

1 tbsp. of chopped thyme

2 tbsp. of dark beef stock

1 tbsp. oil

1 small knob of butter

salt and pepper

FOR THE POMME PURÉE

2 lb. maris piper potatoes, peeled, steamed, then riced or put through a manual food mill

½ lb. butter

½ c. heavy cream

salt and white pepper to taste

FOR THE PEPPERCORN SAUCE

½ c. of good reduced beef jus

¼ c. port

1 tbsp. redcurrant jelly

1 tbsp. cognac

1 tbsp. green peppercorns

salt and white pepper

___

METHOD

FOR THE POT KILN MARINADE

Whiz these all up in a food processor until livid green, then apply generously to the T-bones and cutlets as a marinade—it will protect the meat and taste delicious when grilled.

TO MAKE THE KROMESKI

Brown the venison shoulder/neck well in a little oil, fry vegetables in the same pan then cover with liquid and cook for 6 hours at 250°F.

Then remove the venison and flake ready to make Kromeski.

Sweat the shallots and thyme in a little oil and butter, then add the flaked venison. Mix with the stock and season to taste. Roll into a sausage with plastic wrap, and place in fridge for 4 hours or overnight.

Cut into ½ inch rounds and breadcrumb as usual - I like panko crumbs.

Deep fry at 350°F for 4 min.

FOR THE POMME PURÉE

Bring the butter and cream to a simmer in a heavy pan, then add the riced potatoes a handful at a time. Whisk gently over a low heat until super smooth and silky. Season and put aside.

FOR THE PEPPERCORN SAUCE

Reduce the beef jus by another two-thirds, and do the same in another pan with the cognac and port, until you are left with a couple of tablespoons. Add the reduced alcohol to the glace [reduced jus], and season.

Bring a grill pan up to heat, and place the marinated T-bones on it, cooking them for 2 min a side. Remove them from the heat and place in a 375°F oven for 3 min. Grill the chops for 2 min a side, then rest both meats for 3 min.

TO PLATE

Place the pomme on the plate together with a handful of buttered green beans or savoy cabbage.

Place the chops and T-bone over the pomme and anoint with peppercorn.

Yum . . .

FORMER PUPILS OF WESTMINSTER KINGSWAY COLLEGE

Anyone who enjoys cooking will at some point pass on that knowledge to someone else, whether it is a grandparent teaching their grandchildren to make scones or a parent sharing cooking tips with their children: we all enjoy passing on what we know. It therefore comes naturally to all chefs to pass on their knowledge to other chefs, and I've done so throughout my career, from my first week as a lecturer at the Westminster Kingsway College, to the present day.

When I was a student at the college myself, I had the pleasure of being taught by many fantastic lecturers including Barry Jones, Michael Hollingsworth, Ken Fraser MBE, Colin Selwood and Colin Stone. I have never forgotten what they taught me and to this day I am grateful for their generosity in patiently passing on their phenomenal knowledge. I have great memories of being at college and little did I know I would end up back working at the place where everyone becomes a part of the Westminster family for life.

The lecturers there all form part of a team which has the pleasure of teaching many students who go on to work in top establishments all over the world. It makes me extremely proud to have taught these guys and to have played a small part in their careers.

Here we have a small selection of some of these former students who have gone on to become great ambassadors for our industry. In their professional lives, in restaurants and on TV shows, these chefs all use venison and the wild food from Britain's natural larder. Most importantly, they all have a knowledge about its provenance, a deep respect for it as a product and a keen appreciation of how to prepare and cook it.

Venison neck tagliatelle with wild mushrooms and celeriac purée

Serves 6

SONNY LEE

Sous Chef at Wragge Lawrence Graham & Co International Law Firm

I have loved game, and venison in particular, from a young age. To know that a deer has lived a wild, free life with little interference from humanity, and the fact that throughout history it has been hunted and eaten for food is what excites me the most. But it wasn't until I attended one of José's game demonstrations at Westminster Kingsway College that I truly started to understand and appreciate this animal. After this demonstration I talked to José and decided to attend the college full-time, enrolling that year. For the next three years I worked closely with José as my mentor during which time my passion and understanding of venison grew. Since leaving college I have kept in close contact with José, attending hunts and other game events with him,

where I continue to learn more about the wonders of venison. Today I still use the knowledge José gave me, when I'm designing my recipes and menus.

INGREDIENTS FOR BRAISED VENISON NECK RECIPE

Braised venison neck

2 lb. rolled and tied venison neck filet cut into two

2 medium carrots peeled and chopped

3 sticks of celery chopped

1 large onion peeled and chopped

½ a large leek chopped

1 small purple beetroot peeled and chopped

4 oz. tomato purée

5¼ c. of a good dark chicken or venison stock (stock cubes won't work)

5 cloves of garlic, crushed

2 sprigs rosemary

4 sprigs thyme

2 bay leaves

10 juniper berries

10 black peppercorns

1 bottle of red wine

2 tbsp. of vegetable oil

salt to taste

METHOD FOR BRAISED VENISON NECK

In a saucepan big enough for all the ingredients, heat up the vegetable oil, season the venison neck with salt, then fry, turning occasionally until evenly browned all over, then remove from the pan and set aside.

In the same pan fry the carrots, celery, leeks, onion and garlic until a good color then add the tomato purée and cook out for a minute or two (be careful not to burn the tomato purée as this will give the dish a bitter taste)

Add the rest of the ingredients along with the seared venison neck, then cover and simmer for about 4 hours or until you can put a knife through without any resistance.

Remove the neck and strain the remaining liquid to remove any bits, then place the liquid back on the stove and reduce by 75% until the stock is a nice sauce consistency, skimming occasionally to remove excess fat. Put aside.

With the venison neck, remove the string and then shred or finely chop, then put aside.

CELERIAC PURÉE RECIPE

10 oz. peeled celeriac (celery root), small dice

¼ c. heavy cream

1 tsp. olive oil

pinch of salt and pepper

METHOD FOR PURÉE

Put the chopped celeriac in a baking tray with the olive oil and salt, mix with your hands until evenly coated.

Cover the tray with tin foil and cook in the oven at 325°F for 30 min or until you can squash the largest piece of celeriac with ease.

In a food processor add the celeriac and double cream, blitz until a purée, then salt to taste.

Pass through a fine sieve to remove any lumps and set aside.

TO GARNISH

2 oz. fresh tagliatelle per person

7 oz. cleaned girolles (or other wild mushroom in season)

2 tsp. butter

⅓ oz. parsley, chopped

venison sauce

chopped/shredded venison neck

celeriac purée

salt and pepper to taste

In a saucepan heat the butter then fry the mushrooms until golden, add the chopped venison and the remaining venison sauce.

In a separate pan of boiling salted water, cook the fresh tagliatelle.

In another pan, heat the celeriac purée and keep warm.

Once the pasta is cooked, add it into the pan with the venison, add the chopped herbs. (Add some of the pasta water if you need to let the sauce out a bit so it coats the pasta nicely.)

To plate up the dish, place the celeriac purée and venison tagliatelle on the plate by either putting the purée under the pasta or in a bowl to be served separately.

Venison, beetroot, orange and hazelnut and brussel salad

SOPHIE WRIGHT

Owner of Sophie Wright Catering, author of *Home at 7, Dinner at 8* and other cookery books

I was first introduced to the joys of venison and cooking venison while at Westminster Kingsway College, where I was taught by José. During my time at college, I was lucky enough to be able to work with some of the best products and ingredients the UK had to offer and the lecturers always made the effort to ensure we were exposed to as many different elements of the culinary world possible. I well remember the first time we witnessed a deer being skinned and broken down into its various cuts. It was utterly fascinating and I was inspired by the countless possibilities this beautiful animal had to offer an enthusiastic young chef.

José was always passionate about venison and game and made it possible for us students to skin, prepare and cook them all on a regular basis.

Venison, when in season, is always a staple on my menus. I love helping to change people's perception of game in general, encouraging them to love it as much as I do.

INGREDIENTS

¾ lb. top round venison, all sinew removed

Black pepper and salt

2 tbsp. rapeseed oil

FOR THE SALAD

4 oz. beetroot, raw, very thinly sliced

2 large oranges, segmented

½ c. toasted hazelnuts

5 oz. brussel sprouts, raw, very thinly sliced

2 oz. breakfast radishes, very thinly sliced

½ tbsp. flat leaf parsley, roughly chopped

DRESSING

1 tbsp. wholegrain mustard

1 tbsp. runny honey

1 tbsp. apple cider vinegar

¾ c. rapeseed oil

⅓ c. hazelnut oil

METHOD

Preheat oven to 400°F.

Drizzle the venison in oil and coat generously in black pepper and sea salt.

Pour the remaining oil into a large frying pan and turn the heat to high. Lay in the pepper-crusted venison and seal on all sides until well browned and caramelized.

Remove from the pan, transfer to a tray and finish cooking in the oven for 6-8 min then remove from the oven and leave to rest while you make the salad.

Mix the shaved beetroot with the orange segments, the shaved brussel sprouts and the radishes in a bowl. Add the parsley and the toasted hazelnuts.

Now make your dressing. Mix the wholegrain mustard with the honey and the vinegar. Slowly add both the oils and whisk until the dressing is emulsified. Season with salt and pepper.

Pour half the dressing over the salad and mix well. Taste and season with salt and pepper.

Portion the salad and slice the venison. Lay the venison on top and drizzle over a final bit of dressing.

Venison steaks with garlic mash and roasted sweetcorn

Serves 4

HENRY HERBERT
Hobbs House Bakery. One of the Fabulous Baker Brothers TV series

There is something special about deer. It conjures up images of dusky woodland, misty ponds and autumn leaves: the last noble beast of England. If you get the opportunity to go out with a gamekeeper and stalk one, you will know what it is to be silent while nature buzzes around you, as you hunt the prey. This is what makes venison so special. It has grown rich on the pastures of the land. Wild herbs and berries give the meat a unique taste and with a few simple ingredients you can have a feast fit for any table. Here is one of my favorite ways to cook a venison steak. Just don't be tempted to over-cook it.

José Souto was one of my teachers throughout my three years at Westminster College. The larder and butchery kitchen plays such an important role in any restaurant and is so often over-looked. It is testament to my time at Westminster College that I went on to run my own butcher's shop, so something must have stuck. Working in José's kitchen was the only time I've seen and eaten a wild goose. José's enthusiasm for wild food and for curing and smoking passed on to me and it is something that I have also become passionate about. I look back at my time at Westminster with fondness and with the knowledge that I was taught by some of the best teachers around.

INGREDIENTS

4 venison haunch steaks

salt and pepper

rapeseed oil

sprig of rosemary

knob of butter

SWEET & SOUR ONIONS

2 onions thinly sliced

sprig of thyme

rapeseed oil

4 tbsp. white wine vinegar

2 tbsp. medlar or redcurrant jelly

GARLIC MASH

2 lb. desirée potatoes

4 cloves of garlic

⅓ c. milk

5 oz. butter

salt and pepper

ROAST SWEETCORN

1 corn on the cob

rapeseed oil

knob of butter

sprig of rosemary

salt and pepper

METHOD

To make the sweet and sour onions, gently sweat the onions and thyme in a little oil for 5 min until soft but not colored. Pour in the vinegar and jelly and cook for 5 min until syrupy and glossy. Season and keep warm.

Season the venison well. Heat a large frying pan and add the oil. Brown the steaks on each side for 3 min, to make a nice brown crust. Turn the heat down and add the rosemary and butter. Baste the steak with the foaming butter then remove and rest for 5 min before slicing thinly.

Use the steak pan to make a quick sauce. Put back on the heat and add a small glass of red wine. Boil and scrape the bits off the bottom. Add a dollop of redcurrant jelly and a glass of chicken stock. Reduce and season.

To make the mash, cut the potatoes in half and boil in plenty of water with the skins on and with the whole cloves of garlic until soft. Drain and allow to steam off. Push the potato through a ricer into a pan containing the warm milk and butter. Beat and season.

Rub a little salt on the corn cob kernels. Fire up a gas stovetop burner and carefully char the outside of the cob, using tongs to turn it until nicely browned for that sweet charred taste. Use a knife to cut the kernels off when cooked but not mushy. Heat a pan and foam the butter with the rosemary sprig. Add the sweet corn, season and cook for 4 min.

Serve the garlic mash, onions and roasted sweetcorn with the sliced venison. Spoon some sauce over.

Spiced venison pastilla, fennel seed yoghurt & pomegranate dressing

Serves 4

SELIN KIAZIM

Peter Gordon's former Head Chef, Young Spanish Chef of the Year 2010, finalist Young Chef of the Year 2010, 2011

It was 2008 and I remember my introduction to game very well, in the first few months of college. Our class was very fortunate as José was doing a talk on various game along with a demonstration to a more advanced class. I remember finding the whole thing fascinating, but as he was skinning a hare, the room suddenly got very hot and the next thing I fainted into the arms of another lecturer! The only time I have ever fainted, so embarrassing!

Anyway, venison is my favorite game meat. So versatile and under-used as an everyday meat and I hope that José's inspiration will get everyone using it more. I for one have found all that I learnt from José to be incredibly useful in my career,

mainly because thanks to his tuition, I haven't been scared to use venison and have tried to cook all the cuts and not just the loin, now that I have been taught about all venison's glory!

I am currently on my way to opening my own modern Turkish restaurant, where I can't wait to experiment with venison cooked over charcoal and wood.

INGREDIENTS

¾ lb. venison haunch, diced

4 shallots, finely sliced

4 garlic cloves, finely crushed

2 inch ginger, peeled and finely chopped

1 tsp. ground cumin

1 tsp. ground cinnamon

1 tsp. ground cloves

1 tsp. chili flakes

2 oz. blanched almonds, toasted & roughly chopped

2 oz. sultanas or golden raisins

3 oz. chicken stock

½ bunch coriander, finely shredded

4 sheets filo pastry

2 tbsp. butter, melted

¼ c. plus 2 tbsp. icing sugar

2 oz. strained yoghurt

1 tbsp. ground fennel seeds

½ pomegranate, seeds only

4 tsp. pomegranate molasses

3 tbsp. extra virgin olive oil

2 sprigs thyme, picked

salt and pepper to taste

sunflower oil for cooking

METHOD

Drizzle a little oil into a large hot frying pan and add the venison, browning it on all sides and then add the shallots, garlic and ginger, continue to cook for a few minutes.

Now add the spices and cook for another 2-3 min. Finally add the almonds, sultanas, seasoning, chicken stock and ¼ c. of icing sugar. Tip the whole lot into an ovenproof dish, cover with foil and place into a pre-heated oven at 325°F for approximately 90 min. Check after one hour to see if the meat is tender and falling apart. Once cooked, all liquid should be evaporated, if not, just drain it off.

Shred the meat and give everything a good mix, check the seasoning for salt and sweetness. Once the mix is cool add in the coriander and divide the mix into 4.

Take a sheet of filo pastry, brush with melted butter and fold in half. Place one ball of the venison mix into the center of the sheet, and shape into a sausage shape. Brush again with butter, fold in from both sides and then roll up so it resembles a sausage roll. Repeat the process with the rest of the mix. Brush the tops of the pastilla with butter and bake in a pre-heated oven at 375°F for 12 min or until golden brown.

Just before serving lightly dust the tops of the pastilla with icing sugar.

Mix the yoghurt with the ground fennel and a little salt.

To make the pomegranate dressing, whisk the pomegranate seeds, pomegranate molasses, thyme and olive oil, and add a little salt.

To serve, place a pool of yoghurt on each plate and a pastilla cut in half *(see picture)*. Drizzle with the pomegranate dressing.

Enchanting woods at first light

Venison scotch eggs with pickled cucumber and port-poached redcurrants

Serves 4

TOM EGERTON

Executive Chef
Grosvenor House Hotel, Dubai

Venison is not a meat that I often get a chance to work with or eat since I moved to Dubai 7 years ago, so whenever I am back in the UK, I love to experience its rich, slightly gamey flavor and fine texture.

Of course in Britain customers and chefs are used to the lean, dark red venison filet which is easy to prepare, cook and eat but there are lots of other great venison cuts to enjoy. With a bit more fat, resulting in extra flavor, other cuts from the rump or the leg are great to use and are often a lot cheaper than the more popular primary first cuts.

In my recipe of venison scotch eggs, I have used minced venison, which has great flavor and works well with the pickled cucumber and poached redcurrants. As venison is a fairly lean meat I have added some streaky pork bacon which adds juiciness from the pork fat to the mince.

With health and dietary requests in restaurants becoming more and more common, I believe the demand for venison will continue to increase due to its leaner, healthier credentials when compared to beef. Deer has been hunted for thousands of years and, for many, it is still a way of life. I feel that by continuing the use of traditional meats such as venison, chefs and customers are honoring the tradition of hunting and the responsible control of deer numbers that has been in place for generations.

INGREDIENTS

6 fresh eggs

1 lb. minced shoulder of venison

6 slices of streaky bacon

2 sprigs thyme

1 sprig rosemary

salt and pepper to taste

1 c. flour

1 c. panko breadcrumbs

2 tsp. smoked paprika

1 cucumber

1 tsp. turmeric

2 oz. apple vinegar

¼ c. caster sugar

¾ c. port wine

1 c. redcurrants

1 quart vegetable oil

METHOD

FOR THE SCOTCH EGG

Place 4 eggs (cold from the fridge) in a pan of cold water. Bring to a boil and when the water just starts to boil, turn to a simmer, start the timing and cook the eggs for 5 minutes.

Cool the eggs under cold running water and carefully peel the shell, making sure not to break into the egg.

Take the venison, streaky bacon, picked and chopped fresh thyme and rosemary and mince all together in a grinder on a medium coarse die.

Add freshly ground black pepper and salt and mix well. Test a small amount of the meat for seasoning by cooking in a pan.

Split the minced venison into 4 and flatten out. Place the egg in the center and fully cover and seal the egg in the venison mince.

Now time to pane (breadcrumb) the eggs. Mix the smoked paprika with the flour and dust each egg, shaking to remove excess flour. Place into the remaining beaten eggs, then into the finely blended panko crumbs. Repeat the egg and breadcrumb stage.

FOR THE PICKLED CUCUMBER

Peel and remove the seeds from the cucumber and dice into small cubes.

In a dry pan add the turmeric and sugar, dissolve the sugar and as soon as it starts to caramelize, carefully add the vinegar to make a sharp, sweet pickling liquor.

Remove from the heat and add the diced cucumber.

FOR THE PORT-POACHED REDCURRANTS

Reduce the port in a pan until it is a quarter of its original volume. The consistency should be thick but still movable and able to run. Add the redcurrants and remove from the heat, stirring just to warm them.

TO FINISH THE DISH

Heat the vegetable oil to a medium temperature in a pan or to 375°F for a deep fat fryer.

Carefully drop the scotch egg in the oil and cook for around 3 minutes until the breadcrumbs are golden brown and the meat is cooked.

Slice in half and serve with the pickled cucumber and the port-glazed redcurrants. The yolk of the egg should still be soft but warm. If you prefer your eggs fully cooked, boil them for longer in the first step.

Venison burger, pulled venison scrag and herb mayo

(NECK)

Serves 10

WILLIAM HORSWILL

Executive Head Chef, Burger & Lobster

Since leaving Westminster Kingsway College in late 2008, I have worked in three kitchens, all of which have used venison to its full potential. Chapter2 in Blackheath and Chapter1 just outside Bromley used venison in high volume when in season. Andrew McLeish, the chef at Chapter1 is a great advocate of venison and a keen stalker, so the sight of a freshly-shot deer would be commonplace at Chapter1. We would all help with the cleaning, skinning and the butchery of the animal. The best thing about seeing and using the whole animal is that you feel obliged to use every part of it. It also challenges the chef in many ways.

My time at Westminster Kingsway was between 2005-2008. I remember how none of us had a clue when we started what was involved in being a chef. During our time at the college and especially in the second and third year, we were tested well and placed in a real kitchen environment where everything we produced ended up in one of the college restaurants, either the brasserie or the Escoffier room.

The butchery was a fantastically enjoyable area to work in. José would go into great detail about game, both feather and fur: its preparation and cookery as well as its story and provenance. This knowledge has stayed with me throughout my career.

PATTY

3 lb. venison shoulder

1 lb. pork back fat

(75% meat to 25% fat)

Minced once through a 4mm hole. Average ¼ lb. for each patty. Form into a ball and reserve. Do not handle excessively so that the burger will be tender when eaten.

PULLED VENISON SCRAG

2 lb. scrag (neck) of venison, off the bone but uncut

⅔ c. onion, roughly chopped

⅔ c. carrot, roughly chopped

⅔ c. celery, roughly chopped

⅔ c. leek, roughly chopped

4 juniper berries

4 black peppercorns

2 good sprigs thyme

1 good sprig rosemary

1 bay leaf

veg oil

2 c. red wine

1 quart venison stock

METHOD

Combine all the above except the stock and oil, marinate for 24 hours.

Remove all ingredients from the marinade.

Fry the meat in some hot oil until well colored on all sides then remove from pan and fry the veg in hot oil to color well.

Bring the red wine from the marinade to a boil, skim to remove any impurities that float to the top then add the stock and bring to a boil.

Place meat and vegetables into the boiling liquid, then turn down to a simmer, cover with a lid and cook slowly until meat is tender. You could alternatively cook it in the oven at 375°F until cooked.

Remove meat from cooking liquid in one piece, strain the liquid and discard the veg and aromats.

Reduce the cooking liquid until it thickens to the consistency of double cream, skimming.

Separate the meat into long strands with two forks.

When the cooking liquid is reduced, add it to the meat, season and keep warm.

HERB MAYONNAISE

1 c. flat leaf parsley

1 c. chervil

2 egg yolks

½ c. veg oil

½ c. light olive oil

1 tbsp. Dijon mustard

½ c. chives, chopped

Place the yolks, mustard, parsley and chervil in the food processor and blend. Then slowly add the two oils. Remove the finished mayo and add the chopped chive.

TO SERVE

Use a cast iron/heavy-based frying pan to achieve a good crust on the burger.

Season the ball of venison meat well. Add the ball to the hot pan and push to the thickness of approx ¾-inch, allowing cracks in the meat which create more surface area and more roasted, crispy edges to the burger. It will also look hand-made and not machine-made.

Cook until medium rare.

Split the bun, butter the cut sides and toast the cut side down in a separate pan.

Re-heat the pulled scrag in a sauce-pan on the stove.

Place on the bun, firstly the herb mayo, then the burger, then the pulled scrag. Spread a small amount of herb mayo on the other half of the bun before placing on top.

Serve it with triple cooked chips (maris piper, or russet potatoes, with skin on and tossed in parmesan).

Neck of venison 'sausage roll' with tandoori mayonnaise and salad

Serves 4

BEN MURPHY

Young National Chef of the Year 2012, WorldSkills Gold medal winner 2011, protégé of Pierre Koffmann

In 2008 I had the privilege of being taught by one of the most well-informed chef lecturers in the field of butchery, game, poultry and fish at Westminster Kingsway College: José Souto, a truly respected chef. A year later I was lucky enough as a student to go with Mr Souto to Norfolk where I had the opportunity to learn about the different aspects of deer stalking.

Witnessing a deer being shot from distance - Wow! - something you don't see every day, then the preparation of the carcass and all the stages involved until the venison is sold in the shops. It was truly inspiring.

INGREDIENTS

OAT CRUST

2 c. oats, semi-toasted

1¾ c. plain flour

½ c. butter diced

1 sprig lemon thyme

¼ c. water

MINCE FILLING

1 lb. neck of venison

2 slices of white bread

½ c. milk

1 sprig lemon thyme

1 sprig of rosemary

salt and black pepper

TANDOORI MAYONNAISE

2 egg yolks

2 tsp. Dijon mustard

1 c. sunflower oil

1 oz. tandoori powder

1½ oz. ginger

3 oz. lime juice

¾ c. spring onions (scallions), chopped

¾ c. coriander (or cilantro), chopped

1 hard-boiled egg—finely grated

MIXED SALAD

(your own preference) but I like to use frisée/coriander leaves/rocket

METHOD

THE MINCE FILLING

Using the milk cold, soak the bread until a paste. Finely mince or blend the neck of venison, then finely chop the herbs and combine all ingredients in a bowl. Season with salt and pepper. In a restaurant we would normally do a test, which means pan frying some of the meat to make sure seasoning is perfect.

The oat crust is a very similar technique to making a short crust pastry. Toast the oats very lightly until just colored, because once the venison sausage roll is in the oven, the oats will cook further. Crumb the flour and butter together until a really thick dough. Stir in oats then add water to 'let it out' (enough to roll). When formed into a fat 'sausage roll' cook at 375°F for 10 min then 325°F for 12 min.

Mayonnaise's art is not to split the eggs and oil. Whisk the eggs and mustard for minimum 3 min, then pour in the sunflower oil slowly as you whisk. It will soon get thick—the thicker the better.

In a separate bowl, blend all the other ingredients of the mayonnaise together, apart from the coriander, to a dark red tandoori paste. Mix with the thick mayonnaise, pass through a sieve and add the finely-chopped coriander. I grate an egg because I feel it adds another healthy dimension to this dish.

The salad is your own preference. I feel that frisée, rocket and coriander work best because of their sharp flavors and give a good balance to this dish.

155

Pulled venison shank and split pea pie

Serves 4

MARK FROYDENLUND

Head chef, Marcus at the Berkeley Hotel

Here in Britain we are very fortunate to have several great food seasons to look forward to each year: spring lamb, asparagus in May, and in late summer the Glorious 12th and with it, venison. This fantastic game provides me as a chef with so much inspiration and as the winter draws in, the deep flavors of the meat and its hearty nature fit perfectly with the changing weather outside.

One of the many things I love about cooking is that every season is different: culinary discoveries are always being made; there's not always a right or wrong way, all things should be questioned and experimented with. It's only in the last few years that I discovered muntjac, a really special animal and one to be appreciated, and faced the challenge of breaking down the carcass.

My knowledge and respect for venison was initiated by José Souto. I first met José during my time at Westminster Kingsway College, where he was my first lecturer. His passion for venison and all game was clear. One particular visit arranged by José to see both wild and farmed venison during my early training is something that has stayed with me. At college you are only able to scratch the surface of subjects like this, so José's depth of knowledge on a topic as broad as this is something of which his students should take great advantage.

INGREDIENTS

4 medium-sized venison shanks

1 c. butter

½ c. corn starch

2 celery sticks small dice

2 carrots, small dice

1 onion, finely chopped

2 tsp. chopped fresh rosemary

4 star anise

1 tsp. juniper berries

3 tbsp. tomato paste

½ c. Worcestershire sauce

2 c. red wine

1 quart veal stock

1 quart venison or game stock

1 tsp. smoked paprika

⅔ c. split yellow peas

salt and pepper

METHOD

Flour the meat and brown well in ¼ c. of the butter, season.

Remove meat from pan and add another ¼ c. of butter followed by the vegetables: brown these well. Add tomato paste and cook for a further 10 min. Add herbs, and Worcestershire sauce.

Cover with wine, bring to a boil for 5 min then add the two stocks and again bring to boil. Then either cook in a pressure cooker for 90 min or cook on stove just simmering. In both methods cook until the meat is coming away from the bone in strands similar to pulled pork. Once the meat is cooked, strain the liquid, and reserve both liquid and vegetables.

Place split peas in some cold salted water and bring to a boil until soft and cooked then strain and put on one side and keep warm.

Pick the meat off the bones, removing any fat and connective tissue then add to vegetables.

Take half of the braising liquid from cooking the meat and bring to a boil, reduce by half and then add to this the meat and vegetables.

Take the other half of the braising liquid add it to the cooked split peas, season with smoked paprika and finish with a ½ c. butter folded in to peas and season. The peas will break up to form a lovely rich pease pudding.

Allow pease pudding and meat mix to cool.

TO MAKE THE HOT WATER PASTRY

4 c. flour

¾ c. water

½ c. butter

⅓ c. lard

1 tsp. ground juniper

1 tsp. salt

Bring the water, butter, lard, juniper and salt to a boil. Add the liquid to the flour and combine well. Form into a ball and allow to rest.

Once slightly cooled, roll out into a rough rectangle and chill.

BUILDING THE PIE

3 tbsp. chopped parsley

2 x 2 bone venison rack joints

1 egg

Seal the racks well in a smoking hot pan, season with salt and pepper.

Place a layer of the pease pudding at the base of your deep pie dish then place the racks in the center of the pie interlocking the bones from the racks so they support each other.

Next add a layer of the meat and vegetables around the rack with a little chopped parsley, followed by another layer of pease pudding, then meat and parsley, until you reach the top of the dish.

Form a lid with the pastry, piercing the pastry with the bones but once the lid is in place, remold the pastry around the bones.

Trim away any excess pastry and crimp the edges then glaze with egg wash.

Bake at 350°F. until the pastry is well colored, around 20-25 min. By this time the rack should be cooked to a perfect medium rare.

To serve, cut into the crust then take a spoonful of the pie for each serving, remove the racks and cut them into 4 cutlets. Serve one cutlet with each serving of pie.

ACKNOWLEDGMENTS

THE ESTATES

Over eight years of work has gone into this book, with Steve and I travelling around the country stalking and cataloguing different deer species. We could not have put this book together without the help of the Estates who allowed us to roam freely over their lands, capturing the massive archive of photography which went into this book. Steve and I would both like to thank them for their help and patience. We hope they enjoy reading this book as much as we enjoyed putting it together.

HOUGHTON HALL ESTATE

Houghton Hall in Norfolk is where our story started, within the beautiful parkland with its famous herds of white fallow deer.

Our thanks go to Lord Cholmondeley for allowing us to work on the Estate throughout the seasons, in the wild as well as within the park where we looked at all six of the species found in the UK. In particular, a massive thanks must also go to my good friend Julian Stoyles, Houghton's Deer Park manager. Believe me when I say that if it were not for Julian, we would never have completed this book. He is a world authority on everything to do with deer and stalking and has taught me much about both subjects.

www.houghtonhall.com

THE BUCKHURST ESTATE

On the Buckhurst estate we were fortunate enough to stalk wild fallow deer over open countryside as well as within the ancient woodlands of East Sussex. Our thanks go to the 11th Earl De La Warr for allowing us access to the estate, so that we could see large herds of wild fallow that live there.

We must also thank John Cox, Head Keeper on the Buckhurst Estate for taking us stalking and showing us some of the beautiful East Sussex countryside.

www.buckhurstpark.co.uk

THE ESTATE OF GAIRLOCH

On the west coast of Scotland is the picturesque estate of Gairloch which covers some 60,000 acres of highland moor. I remember sitting on a hillside with Steve about 2,000ft above sea level, looking out across the awesome Scottish Highlands and seeing the regal red stags in the distance.

Many thanks to Duncan Mackenzie of the Gairloch Estate, for allowing Steve and me to explore the Highlands in our attempt to capture its beauty on camera for Venison, The Game Larder. Another person on the Gairloch Estate I would like to thank is my good friend Ronnie Buchan, Head Gamekeeper/Deer Stalker there: a true countryman who is a fount of knowledge as well as a cracking shot.

www.theestateofgairloch.com

WOBURN

In Bedfordshire we travelled to Woburn Abbey, home to the Earls and Dukes of Bedford for nearly 400 years. Over the last century the Estate has become synonymous with deer conservation, particularly of the Milu (Père David's deer) that had become extinct in China by 1894. In 1985, 20 Milu deer from the Woburn herd were repatriated to China where they have thrived and now roam in Hubei outside Beijing.

Our thanks to His Grace Andrew Russell, 15th Duke of Bedford, for allowing us to visit the deer park and estate on many occasions. Thanks also to Dan De Baerdemaecker, Deer Park Manager at Woburn, for taking us out and showing where some of the more elusive species could be found, including the Chinese water deer and muntjac.

www.woburnabbey.co.uk

HOLKHAM HALL

Holkham Hall in north Norfolk is a stunning estate with a phenomenal deer park containing most of the UK deer species. Here we spent many days working on the estate, looking mainly at its large herd of fallow and, in the wild, at muntjac. Our thanks to Viscount Coke for allowing us to discover the wonders of Holkham, and also to Head Gamekeeper Kevan McCaig for taking time out of his busy schedule to show us around the estate and positioning us where we would get the best camera shots.

www.holkham.co.uk

EPPING FOREST

Epping Forest was the former hunting ground of the Kings and Queens of England, its ancient pollarded woodland still much the same today as it was when they hunted and chased deer through the forest.

Here large herds of deer appear and disappear at a moment's notice, and we were able to see the deer's interaction and sometimes conflict with local farmers, the general public and roads in this otherwise built-up part of east London.

Our thanks to the City of London Corporation for allowing us access to the forest and the deer sanctuary - and a big thanks to my friend, Forest Keeper Mick Collins. Mick and I have been friends for many years and he took me on my first ever stalking trip. I have learnt so much from Mick over the years and I regard him as a great authority on deer and deer stalking.

www.cityoflondon.gov.uk

THANKS TO OUR SUPPLIERS & SUPPORTERS

LINCOLNSHIRE GAME

Lincolnshire Game have been a strong supporter of me and the college. The quality and care they take of their product is second-to-none. Both Simon Wilkinson and Tristan Kirk are passionate about what they do and in their mission to educate people about game. Our thanks to Lincolnshire Game for supplying all the venison used in this book.

www.lincolnshiregame.co.uk

FLINT AND FLAME KNIVES

Every cook and chef needs the right tools for the job. Precision, accuracy and quality in knives are of paramount importance. The Flint & Flame range delivers on every level, with stylish and beautifully-crafted knives. Throughout this book I have had the pleasure of using Flint & Flame knives and they have done the job they are designed to do every time. My thanks to Steve Mold for supplying the knives for the book.

www.flintandflame.com

BRADLEY SMOKERS

A Bradley Smoker brings a new dimension to cooking game, with flavor and texture guaranteed. Smoking and curing makes the game season last longer by allowing us to extend the shelf life of venison and to make the most of it when there is a glut of in-season game available. Smoking is a fantastic way to add value and it delivers a different culinary experience. Bradley Smokers are easy to control and I have used them in all the smoking recipes in this book. Many thanks to Brigitte and John Watkins for supplying us with Bradley smokers for use in this book.

www.bradleysmoker.co.uk

THE HUNTSMAN GAME LARDERS

The Huntsman Game Larders are affordable, quality larder fridges which are robust, hygienic and durable. The single door larders are large enough to take two fallow carcasses or four smaller deer—and they are also versatile enough to have a selection of accessories that allow you to use the larder in many different ways. Our thanks to Julie Corker of Angel Refrigeration for supplying the single door Huntsman Game Larder used in the book.

www.angelrefrigeration.co.uk

TASTE OF GAME

Taste of Game is passionate about game meat and encourages the consumer to eat game through great recipes, special offers and delicious game products.

www.tasteofgame.org.uk

Kevan McCaig

Head Keeper at Holkham Hall Estate

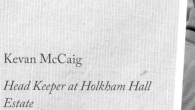

Ronnie Buchan

Head Gamekeeper/Deer Stalker the Gairloch Estate

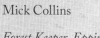

Mick Collins

Forest Keeper, Epping Forest City of London Corporation

Dan De Baerdemaecker

Deer Park Manager at Woburn Estate

John Cox

Head Keeper on the
Buckhurst Estate

Julian Stoyles

Houghton Hall Estate
Deer Park Manager

FURTHER THANKS TO . . .

James Ellis, Gunton Park for spending the day with us at Gunton.

Fergus Williams for allowing us to stalk and photograph roe deer on his land. The resulting pictures make up some of the best roe deer shots in this book.

Ellie and John Savory, Norfolk Quail for introducing me to Fergus and letting me run around their farm, stalking roe at ungodly hours in the morning.

Richard Savory for allowing us to visit his red deer venison farm in Norfolk.

Lee Young and Andy Halford for taking us out stalking in Kent: two of my good stalking and falconry friends.

John Mease, my stalking and falconry buddy—the best eagle man I know, and a fantastic leatherworker: knife sheaths, falconry hoods and many other bespoke items. Thank you for taking me out in Cambridgeshire. Facebook: JM Falconry Hoods.

Ray and Wendy Aliker for allowing Steve and me to invade your beautiful home and do our step-by-step photos.

Gary Hunter for all your support and your words of wisdom on writing books.

The lecturers at Westminster Kingsway College for supporting me and putting up with me going on and on about venison and this book.

Jane Suthering my good friend, for looking over my recipes and editing them, because as she keeps telling me, chefs are great at cooking and doing things on the hoof, but rubbish at writing recipes down properly.

BASC for all their support and a special thank you to Christopher Graffius for starting the ball rolling.

Morris Bond for your support over the years, my friend.

Charlie and Douglas Lee for taking some fantastic footage for our promotional video about this book and thank you to Doug for working the camera when on the odd occasion Steve was on the other side of it - and for clearing up my mess after a cookery shoot.

Annie Tidyman our talented book designer who laid out our work in a way that I could never have imagined, a thousand times better than I expected. Thank you also for being so patient with my ignorance of the design world.

Jo Harris the amazing prop stylist. Thanks, Jo, for your input into this book and for the use of all the amazing props from the collection at Topham Street props. Also thank you to Hannah Bradbury for her input and for tidying up after me.

Ashley Pearman and Russell Staton, and the rest of the Hellfire Club at the Winkleton shoot for the use of the shoot shed and the fantastic spit roast we had there. Also thanks to all the lads who got rather intoxicated and made that shoot so much fun, with amazing pictorial results.

Sarah van Heerden, long-suffering partner of Steve Lee who looked after the dogs and home while I have dragged Steve away on location and she has acted as both referee and judge on more than a few occasions. Thank you Sarah.

And finally, Merlin Unwin Books—to Merlin and Karen for believing in us and working on the amazing book we have all produced.

INDEX